Boomers and Beyond

Reconsidering the Role of Libraries

Edited by
Pauline Rothstein and Diantha Dow Schull

American Library Association
Chicago   2010

Pauline Rothstein has a PhD from Fordham University and an MLS from Pratt. She is an adjunct faculty member at Long Island University's Palmer School of Library and Information Science. At the Palmer School she developed an institute on lifelong learning for older adults that was the catalyst for this book. She is currently program administrator for the LIU/NYU dual degree master's program at New York University. Previously she was dean of the library for Ramapo College of New Jersey and librarian for the Russell Sage Foundation. She has been an active member of the Special Libraries Association and the International Federation of Library Associations. Her firm, TheLibraryDoctor, provides home library services to Boomers.

Diantha Dow Schull established DDSchull Associates to provide advisory services to libraries, museums, and foundations on program development, organizational planning, grantsmanship, and fund-raising. She has served as president of Libraries for the Future (Americans for Libraries Council) and as executive director of the French-American Foundation, director of exhibitions and education at the New York Public Library, director of interpretive programs at the Library of Congress, and assistant director of the Museum Aid Program of the New York State Council on the Arts. Schull holds a master's degree in museum studies from the State University of

New York and is the author of numerous articles on cultural institutions.

The paper used in this publication meets the minimum requirements of American National Standard for Information Sciences—Permanence of Paper for Printed Library Materials, ANSI Z39.48-1992. ⊚

Library of Congress Cataloging-in-Publication Data

    Boomers and beyond : reconsidering the role of libraries / edited by Pauline Rothstein and
       Diantha Dow Schull.

         p.   cm.

    Includes bibliographical references and index.

    ISBN 978-0-8389-1014-6 (alk. paper)

    1. Libraries and older people—United States. 2. Adult services in public libraries—United States.
       3. Aging—United States. I. Rothstein, Pauline M. II. Schull, Diantha Dow.

    Z711.92.A35B66 2010

    027.6'22—dc22   2009025048

ISBN-13: 978-0-8389-1014-6

Printed in the United States of America

14 13 12 11 10   5 4 3 2 1

Contents

Acknowledgments

The concept for *Boomers and Beyond* grew out of a one-week institute for library school students organized by Pauline Rothstein in New York. The institute was modeled on Libraries for the Future's Lifelong Access Libraries Institute, created by Diantha Schull, who agreed to be a presenter. Stephen Abram, who generously gave a full-day presentation, suggested that the presentations would make a good book and recommended that Rothstein contact ALA Editions. While planning the content for the book, Rothstein contacted Schull, who agreed to coedit this volume. The resulting publication draws on our collective knowledge of the library profession and how it could benefit from exposure to new and different perspectives on older adults. We hope that this book will spark new thinking and new practices that contribute to the knowledge base of librarians and others working with older adults.

We owe special thanks to the authors who responded so positively to our invitation to participate in this volume. Each author offers a substantial contribution to library literature and to the literature on aging. At a time when so many people are recognizing the impact of longevity, we believe the chapters in this volume are valuable and unique resources for all who work with older adults.

Introduction

Boomers and Beyond: Reconsidering the Role of Libraries offers a set of new perspectives on aging. It is designed to coincide with growing awareness of the impact of aging on all aspects of American society *and* with the exponential growth in scholarship on aging. These phenomena are due not only to the maturation of the baby boomer generation. They are also due to the growth in the numbers of adults in their 90s or older and the trend for humans to live longer. They challenge librarians and others to explore the implications of extended adulthood on professional practice.

Boomers and Beyond offers a menu of provocative concepts and applications. It is based on three assumptions. First, the lengthening of the human life span will have profound effects on institutions such as libraries. It is not too early for librarians and others to reexamine their understanding of aging and older adults.

Our second assumption is that the library profession can benefit from greater attention to work going on outside the field of library and information science. The field cannot by itself encompass new scholarship on human development and the functioning of the brain, new thinking about "place," or new scholarship on adult education and extended work patterns, to name just a few. Our aim was to reach outside librarianship to a broader field of ideas and scholarship.

Third, we expect that with new information, provocative concepts, and a sense of what may be possible, librarians will be stimulated to use their creativity. At this stage in understanding longevity, how-to manuals may be less useful than concepts that can stimulate experimentation. Each community and each library have different assets, capacities, and needs, and librarians are used to adapting good ideas in their local settings.

Selection of our "unexpected voices" was not a simple task. There is an explosion of theoretical explorations and practical developments around aging in areas ranging from gender, health care reform, and housing to family relationships, mental health, and artistic expression. Our challenge was to identify individuals whose work has specific potential to catalyze new thinking about older adults. In meeting this challenge we found it helpful to think about three distinct categories of exploration.

In part 1, "Older Adults: Essential Concepts and Recent Discoveries," we provide some foundational ideas, an infrastructure for thinking about what Victor and Joanne Marshall call "new patterns of aging." These chapters focus on older adults themselves—what we know about them today and what we are learning about them as their numbers and influence expand. Along with the Marshalls' chapter, "New

Patterns of Aging: Implications for Libraries and Cultural Institutions," the other chapters in this category include "Optimizing Health: A Life-Span Approach," by Margie Lachman and Stefan Agrigoroaei; "Library Leadership for Mature Adult Learners in a Changing World," by Ellie Drago-Severson and Jessica Blum; "The Importance of Spirituality in an Aging Society," by Robert Atchley; and "Work and Purpose after 50," by Stephen Ristau.

In part 2, "Institutional Opportunities," we looked for contributions about how institutions can respond to the new generations of older adults. These chapters include "In Search of Active Wisdom: Libraries and Consciousness-Raising for Adulthood II," by Mary Catherine Bateson; "Information-Questing Moments: Retirement-Age Americans at the Library Door," by Ronald J. Manheimer and Miwako Kidahashi; "Reconsidering Age: The Emerging Role of Cultural Institutions," by Diantha Dow Schull and Selma Thomas; "Reclaiming the 'Public' Library: Engaging Immigrants, Building Democracy," by Nan Kari and David Scheie; and "The Library as Place in an Aging Society," by Diantha Dow Schull.

In our final section, part 3, "Librarians' Perspectives," three librarians bring a variety of experience to the question of how libraries will change in the context of an aging society. These chapters are "Conversations and the True Knowledge of Generations," by R. David Lankes with assistance from Pamela H. Jureller; "Old Dogs, New Tricks: The Myths and the Realities," by Stephen Abram; and "Musings on Challenges for Librarians in 2040," by Pauline Rothstein.

Finally, we should mention that from the outset of our work on *Boomers and Beyond,* we have tried to shape it for multiple uses. One purpose of the volume is to serve as a text for library education. It also offers opportunities for individual enrichment and professional development. As a resource for institutional and service planning, *Boomers and Beyond* will prompt readers to rethink the entire spectrum of services for older individuals.

PART ONE

OLDER ADULTS
ESSENTIAL CONCEPTS AND RECENT DISCOVERIES

NEW PATTERNS OF AGING

Implications for Libraries and Cultural Institutions

Joanne Gard Marshall and Victor Marshall

1

Our purposes in this chapter are to present an overview of the demographic changes occurring in the United States and other developed countries that experienced a baby boom after World War II and to discuss some implications for libraries and other cultural institutions, such as museums. The boomers, born between 1946 and 1964, have had a strong impact on all life stages through which they have lived. The baby boom cohort has always been larger than the age groups ahead of it and those immediately behind. The leading-edge boomers are now in their 60s, and we will see over 70 million of them moving into older adulthood in the United States over the next two decades. The boomers are expected to make their influence felt on everything from health care to lifelong learning and civic engagement. Although the boomers are a diverse group in many ways, there are more active, healthy, and well-educated older adults among the boomers than in any previous cohort. As such, they are likely to redefine what it means to be an older adult and what it means to retire. The term *senior* may have to be traded in for something more colorful, and stereotypes of the elderly will need to change.

Cultural institutions such as libraries and museums will be affected by this demographic shift in many ways. Not only will their clientele be aging but also the library and museum workforce itself. There may be more opportunity for recruiting volunteers but also a need to consider ways in which older adults can receive compensation for their valuable services, especially given the changing economic situation. The sheer number of aging baby boomers will also increase the numbers of disadvantaged older adults who have poor incomes, low literacy, and various sorts of limitations. Libraries and other cultural institutions will need to be attentive to the nature of these shifts so that they can make timely adjustments in their planning, policies, and practices. The enormity of these changes presents both a challenge and an opportunity and calls for a more innovative approach to services to the older adult segment of the population than has usually been the case. Being knowledgeable about the facts behind population aging can help librarians and cultural institution professionals engage in a broader dialogue with potential community partners regarding ways that they can work together to meet the challenges that lie ahead.

We begin the discussion with a concise overview of the aging of the population, with particular attention to demographic and related social aspects that are relevant to policy and practice for libraries and cultural institutions in an aging society. It is important for planners to understand the field of demography and the factors that lead to changes in the age composition of a society. Even more important are the particular changes that are likely to occur in a local community, such as the catchment or service area of a library or museum. Thus, our focus is not on the aging of individuals but rather on the aging of societies and communities. We then describe the aging of U.S. society and the factors that are shaping demographic outcomes.

Demographic analysis can provide the numbers of people in a given category, notably their age bracket and gender. To shape good institutional policy and practice, we need to go beyond those demographic numbers to examine other social factors such as socioeconomic status, educational attainment, and labor force participation. The data will show that the United States has a large and growing number of older adults. Most people over the age of 50 can be referred to as *active older adults,* and sound institutional policy and practice directed to serving active older adults will have to recognize the great diversity among this population.

THE THREE CAUSES OF POPULATION CHANGE AND THEIR IMPACT ON AGE STRUCTURE

Stated simply, if we know three things, we can arrive at the age and gender composition of a society and make reasonable predictions about how this composition will change. These three factors are fertility rate, mortality rate, and migration/immigration patterns. All other things being equal, if the *fertility* rate falls, a population will age as fewer children are born to bring down the average age. Existing larger cohorts (including the very large baby boom cohort born 1946–1964) will grow older, and older people will come to represent a larger proportion of the population. If the *mortality* rate falls, people will live longer, and, all else being equal, the number of people in the older age categories will increase. *Migration* (and immigration) patterns have a more complex effect on the age structure. Immigrants are more often younger adults than older adults. When immigrants come, they often have children. This brings the average age of the population down and lowers the rate of population aging that might otherwise occur because of changes in fertility and mortality of the initial population.

In most countries of the world, including less-developed countries, fertility rates have been falling over the past several decades, and this drop is the major cause of population aging. This pattern is also generally true for the United States, but the overall reduction in fertility has been countered by a more recent upward trend. Current completed fertility rates in the country are about 1.9, compared to 3.1 in 1975, but the current figure reflects a very recent rise from a low of 1.7 in 1980. In contrast, European completed fertility rates are as low as 1.2 or 1.3, and the rate in Canada is about 1.4. Fertility is higher in the United States than in other industrialized countries mainly because of the large Hispanic and Latino/Latina population, which has higher rates than other groups.

The high fertility rates that produced the boomer cohorts born 1946–1964 will soon significantly increase the numbers and proportion of people age 65 and older. Thus, the *percentage* of people age 65+ is projected to rise from 12.7 to 20.2 between 2008 and 2050, and the percentage age 85+ is expected to rise from 1.8 to 4.3 over the same period. The *number* of people over age 65 is expected to rise from just over 35 million to about 70 million between 2008 and 2050, and the population age 85+ is expected to rise from about 4.2 million to about 21 million over this same period (U.S. Census Bureau 2008b).

In the developed countries (with the exception of the former Soviet Union), *mortality* rates have fallen dramatically in the past century. Thus, *life expectancy* has increased, and the populations of these countries have been aging. Until about a half century ago, most population aging in the developed countries could be accounted for by declining fertility, but changes in mortality (and derivative changes in life expectancy) are now the second-greatest cause of population aging. Not only is life expectancy at birth increasing, but life expectancy at advanced ages has also increased dramatically. Life expectancy projections are based on current age- and sex-specific mortality rates. Recently, these projections have resulted in conservative estimates of life expectancy because survivorship at any age has almost always increased. Between 1900 and 2001, life expectancy for women in the United States who reach age 65 increased by more than six years, so that half of those who reach age 65 can expect to reach age 83. For those who reach age 85, life expectancy has increased by two more years, with half of those who reach age 85 predicted to live to 91. Men have also increased their life expectancy over the past century, although they can expect to live fewer years than women.

Very large differences in life expectancy occur not only by sex but also by minority status. For example, projections based on 1998 data show that white females at age 65 had the highest life expectancy, at just over nineteen years, contrasted with a life expectancy of just fifteen years for nonwhite males at age 65. The other two groups fall in between these two groups, with nonwhite females having greater life expectancy than white males (CDC 1998). Despite these strong gender and race differences, however, a dramatic increase in life expectancy exists for all gender/race groups.

Immigration to the United States has had a complex impact on the population's age structure. As mentioned earlier, immigrants are generally younger people who then have children. The large number of Hispanic immigrants to the United States has contributed to a higher fertility rate than in other industrialized societies. If not for the historically high fertility rates in this group, the United States would be a demographically older country. Within-country *migration* patterns have an impact on the demographic structure of regions, states, and smaller communities. Younger people may move great distances, such as to the Sun Belt states or away from the Rust Belt in search of jobs. An upward tick in interstate migration takes place at retirement, as people are no longer tied to their communities by jobs (Frey 2007). However, in general, older adults are less likely to change residence than are other age groups, and less than one-fifth of older adults who do move relocate to another state. This said, there is variability by state, with the Sun Belt states experiencing net gains of people age 65 and older, while most states in the Northeast and Midwest, plus California and Alaska, see more older adults leave than move in (Longino 1995). Taken together, changes in fertility, mortality, and immigration and migration have led to significant changes in the American population age structure and will continue to do so, as shown in table 1.1.

TABLE 1.1   Percent Distribution of the Projected Population by Selected Age Groups for the United States, 2008 to 2050 (Percentage of total resident population as of July 1)

AGE	2008	2010	2015	2020	2025	2030	2035	2040	2045	2050
Total population	100.00	100.00	100.00	100.00	100.00	100.00	100.00	100.00	100.00	100.00
Under 18 years	24.55	24.25	23.99	23.93	23.74	23.51	23.29	23.17	23.14	23.14
Under 5 years	6.83	6.80	6.78	6.69	6.57	6.47	6.43	6.44	6.44	6.41
5 to 13 years	12.03	11.97	11.98	11.95	11.89	11.74	11.60	11.52	11.53	11.55
14 to 17 years	5.69	5.48	5.23	5.29	5.29	5.30	5.26	5.21	5.17	5.18
18 to 64 years	62.73	62.79	61.62	60.02	58.38	57.19	56.80	56.80	56.85	56.69
18 to 24 years	9.83	9.90	9.49	9.03	9.11	9.12	9.16	9.13	9.06	9.01
25 to 44 years	27.27	26.78	26.36	26.28	25.91	25.50	25.15	24.99	25.20	25.25
45 to 64 years	25.62	26.10	25.78	24.71	23.36	22.57	22.49	22.68	22.59	22.43
65 years and over	12.72	12.97	14.39	16.05	17.88	19.30	19.91	20.03	20.01	20.17
85 years and over	1.79	1.85	1.93	1.93	2.03	2.34	2.94	3.50	4.02	4.34

Source: U.S. Census Bureau. 2008b.

Currently, just under 13 percent of Americans are 65 and older. By 2015, the percentage will have risen to 14.4, and by 2030, about one in five Americans is projected to be age 65 or older (Smith 2003; U.S. Census Bureau 2008a; see also Shrestha 2006). According to 2008 census figures, just over a quarter of the U.S. population is ages 25–44, and another quarter (which corresponds closely to the baby boom generation born 1946–1964) is ages 45–64. The percentages of the population in these two categories are projected to remain quite stable until at least 2050, while the percentages in the older age categories (65+ and 85+) will increase dramatically. Even though the percentages are small in the 85+ category, they will be 2.4 times greater in 2050. Looking at numbers rather than percentages, there are currently just under 100,000 centenarians in the United States, but this number is projected to rise to over 800,000 in the next fifty years (Krach and Velkoff 1999). But centenarians are only the dramatic tip of the iceberg of population aging.

DIVERSITY AND AGE

The numbers tell us that there is tremendous diversity within the aging society—by age itself and by gender, race, class, health, and place (rural versus urban). We consider these factors next.

Place

As we noted when discussing migration, the age structure within a given country will vary considerably by place. In the United States, a state will age if its younger members migrate out of state, if older people retire there, or if fertility rates remain low, below replacement levels (we saw that this varies by ethnicity, which is related to differentials among receiving states). As early as 2015, only two states will have less than 11 percent of their populations age 65+. Utah, Texas, Maryland, and Georgia will have populations with less than 13.5 percent age 65 and older. In North Carolina, 16.4 percent of the citizens will be age 65 and older. Florida, which already has an aged population, will reach about 20 percent age 65+, as will Oregon, Montana, and West Virginia. A state population will grow younger if it receives migrants from other states or immigrants from other countries, perhaps attracted by economic development. States vary considerably in being senders or receivers of migrants or immigrants of different ages. Sometimes these features will cancel out: California and Alaska are projected to continue to attract young migrants. Georgia will as well but is also affected by retirement migration (and apparently more so than California). "Aging in place"—the aging of people already in a locality—is much stronger than migration patterns in affecting the age structure of the population (Frey 2007, 11–14).

The same principles operate within states at the community level. Rural areas tend to age more rapidly than urban areas because of a migration of younger people to the cities for higher education and for work. On the other hand, states or areas within states that attract older people as "amenity retirees"—retirees who have resources to pay for special services—will find increases in the older adult population. For example, some rural and coastal or mountainous areas may develop continuing-care retirement communities or attractive leisure-oriented facilities for golf, sailing, and wilderness living (Longino 1995). Migration data, coupled with age structure data, can be used to identify current proportions of seniors, youth, and people in the middle, so migration data should be included in projections for the future.

Gender and Family Status

To properly understand a potential or actual client base for libraries and cultural institutions, it is important to understand that gender differences in life expectancy produce an increasing ratio of women to men as one moves up the age structure. Considering the total U.S. population, about 51 percent are female, but 58 percent of those age 65+ and 70 percent of those 85+ are female (U.S. Census Bureau 2001). In 2000, there were 85.7 men ages 65–69 for every 100 women (a sex ratio of 85.7). The sex ratio falls to 59.0 in the 80–84 age bracket and to 34.0 in the 90–94 age bracket (He et al. 2005, table 2-3, 24). Women outlive men by almost eight years, so most men are able to die in the arms of their spouse, so to speak. Women also tend to be heavy users of libraries and cultural institutions.

Table 1.2 shows marital status for men and women in three of the older age categories in the year 2007. Women ages 65–74 are more than three times as likely to be widowed as are men, and women age 75+ are almost three times more likely to be widowed. The figures for divorce are higher for both men and women in the younger categories, and this is a cohort effect. We can expect that as younger cohorts move into these age categories, they too will have higher divorce rates. Thus, more older women will be living alone in the later years, with a greater likelihood of institutionalization.

TABLE 1.2   Marital Status of U.S. Population Age 55+, by Age and Gender, 2007

	NEVER MARRIED	MARRIED	WIDOWED	DIVORCED
Men				
55 to 64 years old	6.8	74.1	2.2	13.8
65 to 74 years old	4.3	75.6	7.7	9.6
75 years old and over	3.7	69.0	20.0	4.9
Women				
55 to 64 years old	6.6	62.7	9.0	18.4
65 to 74 years old	4.0	54.3	26.2	13.0
75 years old and over	3.4	30.1	58.2	6.3

Sources: Smith 2003 and earlier Current Population Reports; U.S. Census Bureau 2008.

These data also suggest that a lot of older women are providing informal health and social care to their husbands. When women, as widows, need support, they turn first to adult children. A number of studies estimate that of actual care provided to the elderly living in the community, about 75 percent is provided by the so-called informal sector—mostly family members but also some friends. Women provide about 70 percent of such care: they provide the majority of informal caregiving to spouses, and when informal care is provided to a widow, that caregiver is also likely to be a woman. Caregiving is *not* just women's work, as some commentators allege, but it is more often done by women than by men. The type of work done by men and women also differs, with women providing more assistance with personal hygiene, for example, and men more assistance with financial management or transportation. These considerations are relevant for institutional policy and practice for older adults, because they can affect the time and energy as well as flexibility of older adults to engage in community-based activities. As the number of elders who are not mobile increases, libraries will likely find that their home delivery services are in greater demand. Even active older adults will experience increasing limitations that may constrain their activities in family, community, or workplace settings.

Race

Life expectancy also differs by race, and the racial composition of the population is affected by racial patterns of fertility and immigration. In 2006, 19.0 percent of persons age 65+ were minorities. Of these, 8.3 percent were African American, 3.1 percent Asian or Pacific Islander, and less than 1 percent American Indian or Native Alaskan; less than 1 percent listed two or more races. The Hispanic designation may include any race, but 6.4 percent of the older population listed Hispanic origin (Administration on Aging 2007, 6). Race and place often interact. For example, in some states, such as North Carolina, certain rural regions left behind by economic development and certain neighborhoods within cities have high representations of African Americans. As we note later in this chapter, race is also strongly associated with economic and health status throughout the life course and in the older adult years.

Class

The reduction of old-age poverty has been a major accomplishment of American public policy, largely through the introduction and improvement of Social Security. As recently as 1959, 35 percent of older adults (65+) lived below the poverty threshold, and this level far exceeded that of any other age group. Since about 1983, the old-age poverty rate has been roughly equal to that of people ages 18–64, at around 10 percent. In 2005, about 3.4 million older adults (9.4 percent) lived below the poverty line, but another 2.2 million (6.2 percent) were classified as "near-poor" (Administration on Aging 2007, 11). Child poverty rates, once lower than those for people age 65+, have been higher since the mid-1970s (U.S. Census Bureau, Current Population Survey, various years). However, it is probable that poverty in the later years is more stable, while that in childhood is more likely to be transient.

The overall bright picture of reduced poverty among older adults is complicated by considerable variation. In 2006, only 8 percent of family households of those age 65+ had incomes of less than $15,000, but an additional 16.7 percent reported incomes of less than $25,000. Income varies greatly by gender and race. The median income of *persons* age 65+ in 2006 was $23,500 for males but only $13,603 for females. *Households* containing families headed by persons 65+ reported a median income in 2006 of $39,649. However, households headed by non-Hispanic whites reported a median income of $41,091, compared to a median household income of just $30,775 for African American–headed households and $29,385 for Hispanic households. The rate for households headed by those of Asian ethnicity was $43,035 (Administration on Aging 2007, 10).

In addition to income, differences in wealth, or net worth, are important. Wealth is defined as the net economic resources of a household, the value of all assets minus the value of all liabilities. Net worth and its composition vary tremendously over the life course. The median net worth of all U.S. households, *excluding home equity,* in the year 2000 was $13,473. People under 35 had the lowest net worth, with just $3,300 if home equity is not counted. Each age group older than 34 has more net worth until the ages 70–74 category, when it is $31,400. Net worth exclusive of home equity then falls to $19,025 in the 75+ category. When considering these figures, it is important to recognize they represent cross-sectional differences and do not represent the life-course net-worth history of an individual. Home equity makes a very large difference. Including it as part of net worth raises total equity to $7,240 in the under age 35 category, and households in the older age categories show significant increases. In the age brackets of interest here, householders ages 45–54 have a median net worth of $83,150; those ages 55–64, $112,048; those ages 65–69, $114,050; and those ages 70–74, $120,000, following which there is a decline to just $100,100 for those age 75 and older (He et al. 2005, 108). Thus, the home is a key foundation of economic security for older people.

Large gender and ethnic differences in home ownership are apparent in the later years. Home ownership is lower among older people living alone, among females, and among minority groups other than non-Hispanic whites. Thus, in 2001, 83.2 percent of white households were owner-occupied, but only 63.3 percent of black households, 63.3 percent of Asian and Pacific Islander households, and 64.5 percent of Hispanic households were owner-occupied (He et al. 2005, 110–11). Many assets other than the home generate income. These assets include personal savings, stocks and bonds, and certificates of deposit. Thus, many older adults, who are less able to generate income through paid employment, are at risk because of such factors as devaluation of stock portfolios, lower interest rates, and mortgage foreclosure. Economic downturns are likely to affect the older population with limited incomes more than younger workers who have more earning potential.

Health Status

In the past, many stereotypes linked older adults and disabilities even in the services for seniors offered by libraries. But most people remain quite healthy until very late in life. Asked to describe their health as excellent or good versus fair or poor, 19.6 percent of those ages 55–64 rated their health as fair or poor in a national survey, compared with 33.6 percent of adults age 85+. Non-Hispanic, black older adults were more likely than others to report fair or poor health, except in the age 85+ category, and poverty was associated with the poorest health, especially among those ages 55–64 (CDC 2006).

Activity limitations are an important factor in terms of ability to participate in library and museum programming, and these limitations vary considerably by age. For example, 16.5 percent of adults ages 55–64 report difficulty walking one-quarter mile, and this figure rises to 22.4 percent for those 65–74, 34.2 percent for those 75–84, and 46.2 percent for those 85+. Corresponding percentages for limitations in standing for two hours range from 20.3 to 59.6, and the range for sitting for two hours is 10.3 to 16.1 percent. Fully 22.2 percent of adults ages 55–64 report difficulties stooping or bending, and this increases to 29.2 percent for those 65–74, 38.1 percent for those 75–84, and 52.3 percent for those 85+ (CDC 2006, table 2, 18). In addition, many older people have chronic conditions, including hypertension (49.2 percent), arthritic symptoms (36.1 percent), and all types of heart disease (31.1 percent) (Administration on Aging 2007, 12). Health is understandably an issue that older adult patrons bring to libraries and museums, and health conditions and limitations, when present, may require adaptations in modes of service provision.

Changing Labor Force Participation Rates

The last basis of social differentiation we shall consider is labor force participation. Not only are there important differences in labor force behavior by age and gender, but there has been a major change in the general pattern of labor force participation over the past half century. Historical data on labor force participation of men and women for the total labor force (labeled "all" in table 1.3) and in three age groups are presented for the period 1970–2007, with a projection to 2016. To participate in the labor force means to be employed (including self-employed) or to be actively

TABLE 1.3   Civilian Labor Force and Participation Rates with Projections

	PARTICIPATION RATE (PERCENT)[a]							
	1970	1980	1990[b]	2000[b]	2005[b]	2006[b]	2007[b]	2016 projection
Male								
All	79.7	77.4	76.4	74.8	73.3	73.5	73.2	72.3
45 to 54	94.3	91.2	90.7	88.6	87.7	88.1	88.2	86.6
55 to 64	83.0	72.1	67.8	67.3	69.3	69.6	69.6	70.1
65+	26.8	19.0	16.3	17.7	19.8	20.3	20.5	27.1
Female								
All	43.3	51.5	57.5	59.9	59.3	59.4	59.3	59.2
45 to 54	54.4	59.9	71.2	76.8	76.0	76.0	76.0	77.8
55 to 64	43.0	41.3	45.2	51.9	57.0	58.2	58.3	63.5
65+	9.7	8.1	8.6	9.4	11.5	11.7	12.6	17.5

Source: U.S. Bureau of Labor Statistics 2007, 2008; unpublished data.

a Civilian labor force as a percent of the civilian noninstitutional population

b Data not strictly comparable with data for earlier years. See source for details.

seeking work. Some workers, and increasingly so in the older age categories, will be working part time.

These data show an overall slight decline in total male labor force participation from 1970 to 2007, but a large increase in that for women. This increase for all women represents a large jump between 1970 and 1980, a more gradual increase until 2000, and then a leveling off. For men, there were strong decreases in labor force participation between 1970 and 2000 in all of the older age groups, followed by steady but rather slight increases until 2007. The downward trend actually extended from the 1950s until the mid-1980s and reflected a corporate focus on early retirement (before age 65). In 1985, the trend to earlier retirement halted, and retirement age gradually increased. Statutory age for receipt of Social Security began to rise gradually, leading more people to remain working beyond age 65. Women's labor force participation did not follow the pattern of men, as the ideology fostered by the women's movement and a greater concern for gender equity in the workforce (among other reasons) led more women to remain in paid work longer. Thus, the gender gap in labor force participation rates lessened (U.S. Bureau of Labor Statistics 2008). Increases in labor force participation for both men and women who are past age 55 and even past age 65 are noteworthy and reflect, in part, not only the factors just mentioned but also the better health that more people are enjoying well into their advanced years.

We will end the demographic discussion with a word of caution about the rhetoric that sometimes accompanies discussions of population aging. The terminology used to describe age groups often misrepresents what is actually going on from a true demographic perspective. For example, the term *generation* has not one but many precise meanings in scientific discourse and a great many more meanings in lay par-lance, where people speak loosely about the boomers, Gen X, Gen Y, Millennials, and so forth. Most of the generalizations made about these different groups are just that—generalizations—and, upon closer analysis, we find that the picture is much more diverse and complex than these labels would suggest. Many other social and economic factors besides age affect the particular situations in which people find themselves.

Another important factor is that generations move forward in time. Genera-tions grow old and, as they do so, pass through age categories, whether these are single years or informally designated age groups such as childhood, adolescence, young adulthood, and so forth. In terms of setting policies and practices, we urge you to focus attention not on generations but on age groups and on the social and economic factors that affect those groups in your community. The stable but large numbers of people who will be in the age category 45–64 and the growing numbers who will be in the age category or categories beyond that represent an enduring challenge for public service organizations. That the first of these categories (45–64) happens to be occupied by persons born into the baby boom generation is largely incidental to policy and practice, because there will be constant flows of people into and out of the 45–64 category. If libraries are positioned to serve the needs of older adults of various ages, they will be able to better serve not only the boomers as they grow older but also the large and growing numbers of people who will flow, over time, into the age 45+ category and the age 65+ category.

IMPLICATIONS FOR LIBRARY AND CULTURAL INSTITUTION POLICY AND PRACTICE

Throughout this chapter we have pointed out some of the implications for policy and practice for librarians and other cultural institution professionals. Here we will bring these implications together with some suggestions for ways in which libraries and museums can take a proactive approach to renewing their commitment to their older adult clientele and keeping up with demographic changes as they occur. First, we need to deal with our own stereotypes of what it means to be an older adult and avoid the negative stereotypes associated with the deficit model of aging. Approaches that emphasize the assets that older adults bring to the workplace, to the community, and to libraries and other cultural institutions will result in a more beneficial out-come for everyone. Staff training and consciousness-raising discussions on the issues of population aging can change attitudes and prepare the organization to deal with these changes in a positive way.

In keeping with a more optimistic view of the possibilities associated with aging, it is important to realize that libraries and museums will need to enrich the oppor-tunities they offer to older adult volunteers. Many boomers are voracious lifelong learners who want to be engaged in meaningful work and who will not be satisfied with boring or mundane tasks. They are more likely to want more control over their terms and conditions of work and to want to plan and organize their own activities and programs rather than having the library or museum staff decide what should be offered. Boomers do not want to be isolated from other age groups and are often interested in intergenerational programming and opportunities to interact with and mentor younger people. This can lead to some very exciting activities for young and old alike. Taking advantage of the experience of older adults and thinking outside the box in terms of collections, services, and new forms of funding will all be required to take advantage of the possibilities ahead.

Although considerable attention is given by the media to the healthy, wealthy, and wise segment of the boomer population, the numbers show that the boomers are also one of the most diverse age groups in history. Differences in race, ethnicity, education, health, workforce history, and economic status work together to determine the opportunities and limitations that later-life adults have available to them. Cultural institutions can help enrich the lives of the citizens who have contributed so much over the years. To do so requires an appreciation of the particular community you are serving and the demographic characteristics of that community. We recommend that you become familiar with the tools that you can use to develop a demographic profile and use the profile for planning purposes. Update the profile regularly, and use it to monitor changes in the community and their implications for programs and services. Remember that cohorts continue to age and that new plans will be required as the boomers move through their later years.

Because population aging will affect all segments of society, the library can be a resource for other community organizations and groups that need information on this trend to use in their own planning. This represents an opportunity for the library to reach out to potential community partners such as senior centers, retirement communities, support services such as Meals-On-Wheels, AARP, and others so that scarce resources can be used most effectively. Devoting staff (and even volunteer) time to developing, nurturing, and sustaining these partnerships will be an important part of making things work.

Providing access to the Internet and other information technologies is an important role for libraries. Technology can also be used to increase access to museums and other cultural institutions when the mobility of older adults is limited. As community gathering places that tend to be viewed as age neutral, libraries have great potential to offer services that avoid some of the negative stereotypes that we have discussed. They can also provide access to computers and other resources required by older adults who are interested in forging new careers or staying in the workforce part time.

A group worthy of special attention in the older adult category includes those who act as caregivers. Providing health information, including resources on nutrition and exercise, as well as a place to meet and offer social support will be important. As the numbers told us, women are more likely to be widowed and to spend a portion of their later life alone, so the social support and self-help group potential of libraries will grow in importance as the boomers find themselves in need of these services. Special projects, such as recording the living history represented by these later-life individuals, are also possible.

Libraries and other cultural institutions have always prided themselves in their ability to enrich the human experience by providing access to knowledge, culture, and the works of our great thinkers, artists, politicians, and leaders. They also have an increasing reputation as places where community members can come together to learn, support one another, and organize around issues of continuing civic engagement. The potential of these institutions to grow and thrive in an aging society seems endless and will only be limited by our own imagination and energy and by the imagination and energy that we unleash in the older adult community as it grows and continues to share its rich experience with us.

REFERENCES

Administration on Aging. 2007. *A profile of older Americans: 2007.* Washington, DC: Administration on Aging, U.S. Department of Health and Human Services.

CDC Centers for Disease Control and Prevention. 1998. *National vital statistics reports* 47, no. 13 (December 24). www.cdc.gov/nchs/data/nvsr/nvsr47/nvs47_13.pdf.

———. 2006. Health characteristics of adults 55 years of age and over: United States, 2000–2003. *Advance Data from Vital and Health Statistics* 370 (April 11).

Frey, William H. 2007. *Mapping the growth of older America: Seniors and boomers in the early 21st century.* Washington, DC: Brookings Institution. www3.brookings.edu/views/ articles/200705frey.pdf.

He, Wan, Manisha Sengupta, Victoria A. Velkoff, and Kimberly A. DeBarros. 2005. 65+ in the United States: 2005. U.S. Census Bureau Current Population Reports, Special Studies, P23-209. www.census.gov/prod/2006pubs/p23-209.pdf.

Krach, Constance A., and Victoria A. Velkoff. 1999. Centenarians in the United States. U.S. Census Bureau Current Population Reports, Special Studies, P23-199RV. www.census.gov/prod/99pubs/p23-199.pdf.

Longino, Charles F. Jr. 1995. *Retirement migration in America.* Houston: Vacation Publishers.

Shrestha, Laura B. 2006. *The changing demographic profile of the United States* (updated May 5). Congressional Research Service, Washington, DC: Library of Congress. www.fas.org/sgp/crs/misc/RL32701.pdf.

Smith, Denise. 2003. The older population in the United States: March 2002. U.S. Census Bureau Current Population Reports, Population Characteristics, P20-546. www.census.gov/prod/2003pubs/p20-546.pdf.

U.S. Bureau of Labor Statistics. 2007. *Monthly Labor Review.* November.

———. 2008. *Employment and Earnings.* January.

U.S. Census Bureau. 2001. Resident population estimates of the United States, by age and sex. www.census.gov/popest/archives/1990s/nat_age_sex.html.

———. 2008a. America's families and living arrangements: 2007. July. www.census.gov/ population/www/socdemo/hh-fam/cps2007.html.

———. 2008b. 2008 national population projections, table 3. August 14. www.census .gov/population/www/projections/summarytables.html.

———. Various years. Current population survey. www.census.gov/cps/.

OPTIMIZING HEALTH
A Life-Span Approach

Margie E. Lachman and Stefan Agrigoroaei

2

The health of the nation is a central concern, and demographics will play an important role over the next fifty years. Population shifts have been dramatic as the baby boom cohorts (those born between 1946 and 1964) are now ages 45 to 63, and many of them have living parents. Indeed, from 1990 to 2000 the fastest-growing segments of the population were those ages 45–54 and those 90–94. Currently 13 percent of the population is age 65 and older. By 2050 it is expected to be 21 percent (Meyer 2001). Aging is accompanied by an increasing risk of developing health problems (Pleis and Lethbridge-Çejku 2007). Heart disease, cancer, diabetes, arthritis, osteoporosis, and dementia are all more prevalent in later life. If we don't take action, we likely will face an epidemic of disability and neurodegenerative diseases, and the needs for caregiving will reach critical proportions. The good news is there are things we can do now to optimize health for the twenty-first century.

HEALTH PROMOTION

In considering how libraries can help to promote health and well-being throughout life, we adopt a life-span perspective, which holds that growth and development are part of a lifelong process. Throughout life everyone experiences gains and losses in functioning, and the balance shifts over time (Baltes, Lindenberger, and Staudinger 2006). In childhood, there are more gains relative to losses. In midlife the balance begins to change, and in old age the losses begin to outweigh the gains (Heckhausen, Dixon, and Baltes, 1989). Nevertheless, gains persist throughout life, and a key goal is to maximize the gains and minimize the losses.

In this chapter we consider health in a broad context and review what scientific research has told us about ways to optimize health. Our definition of health includes the physical, cognitive, and psychological aspects (see figure 2.1). Concerning physical functioning, we consider the number and intensity of functional limitations caused by health problems. Those with disabilities (e.g., limited mobility due to arthritis) may have to restrict their daily activities. For cognitive functioning, we consider multiple dimensions: memory, reasoning, speed of processing, executive functioning, attention switching, and inhibitory control. These components of cognition are needed to carry out the functions of daily living, such as remembering medication schedules and appointments, planning for meals, and making financial decisions. Psychological well-being is typically assessed by ratings of life satisfaction

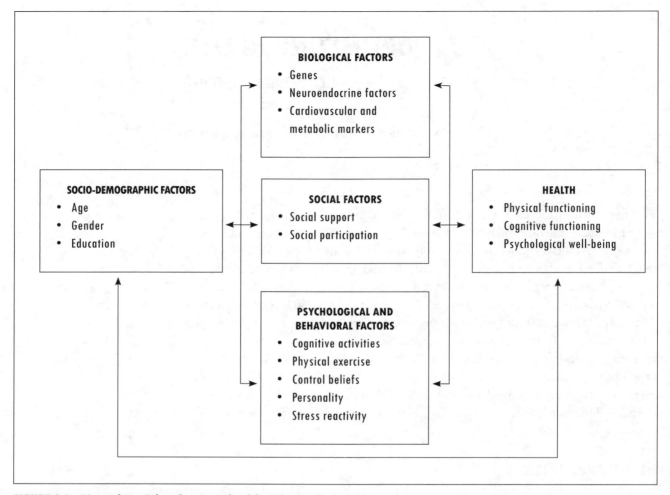

FIGURE 2.1   Biopsychosocial pathways to health with sample variables

or happiness. Based on many studies, we can conclude that the typical trajectory is one of decline for physical and cognitive health starting in midlife (Lachman 2001). In contrast, psychological well-being shows increments over the adult life span and levels off in old age, with some declines late in life (Mroczek and Spiro 2005).

Although on average the patterns of physical and cognitive health trajectories are downward, wide individual differences appear within any age period. This variability is another key feature highlighted in a life-span view (Baltes et al. 2006). Much overlap occurs in the age distributions for all aspects of physical, cognitive, and psychological functioning. In other words, there is often more variation *within* age groups than between groups, showing that chronological age does not necessarily tell the full story. Moreover, this pattern of results raises questions about why some people are able to avoid or delay declines and opens up the possibilities for identifying the sources of these individual differences in patterns of aging. We can explore the protective factors that foster healthy aging and prevent or mitigate declines. We also can begin to identify strategies and lifestyle behaviors to compensate for decrements.

This idea about optimizing aging, however, is not new. A similar message, which implies there are things we can do to bring the aging body and mind under control, was conveyed a long time ago:

> It is our duty, my young friends, to resist old age; to compensate for its defects by a watchful care; to fight against it as we would fight against disease; to adopt a regimen of health; to practice moderate exercise; and to take just enough food and drink to restore our strength and not to overburden it. Nor, indeed are we to give our attention solely to the body; much greater care is due to the mind and soul; for they, too, like lamps grow dim with time, unless we keep them supplied with oil. (Cicero 1946 [44 BC], XI 36)

Although Cicero made these recommendations over two thousand years ago, his prescription for exercise, proper nutrition, and cognitive stimulation remains sound for promoting successful aging (Rowe and Kahn 1998; Vaillant 2002). Yet, there is still much to be done to encourage wider adoption of these and other adaptive behaviors. Recent data (National Center for Health Statistics 2007) show that in 2006, 40 percent of adults age 18 and older did not engage in any leisure time physical activity, and 53 percent of those over the age of 65 were physically inactive. Between 2000 and 2004, among adults 20 to 74 years of age, 66 percent were overweight and 32 percent were considered obese (National Center for Health Statistics 2007). And apropos stimulating the mind, a recent study by the National Endowment for the Arts found that fewer than half (47 percent) of Americans age 18 or older had read a novel, short story, play, or poem in 2002 (Mehegan 2004). This is not surprising given findings from the National Assessment of Adult Literacy. In a survey conducted in 2003 involving more than 18,500 Americans age 16 and older, researchers found that 1 in 7 adults in the United States have low literacy skills and cannot read anything more challenging than a children's picture book or understand medication side effects on a bottle (National Center for Education Statistics 2003). This situation appears to be worse than before. A comparison of data from 1992 and 2003 showed that an additional 3.6 million were classified as low literacy over this period, which is likely to have consequences for health and independent living as these adults grow older.

Much evidence shows that the course of aging is not completely determined by genes. Since Cicero's time, much progress has been made in optimizing aging, including increased longevity and some reduction in disability rates (National Center for Health Statistics 2007). As Cicero believed, modifiable factors, including beliefs and behaviors, can make a difference.

TAKING CONTROL OVER HEALTH AND AGING

In what ways can we control health and aging? We can make a difference through lifestyle choices and healthy behaviors such as exercise, stress reduction, mental stimulation, and adaptive beliefs. Although there are multiple determinants of aging outcomes, the sense of control is one core set of beliefs related to actions and behaviors (Bandura 1997). *Control* refers to beliefs about abilities and opportunities to bring about desired outcomes as well as expectancies for losses and gains. Those who have a high sense of control strongly believe there are things they can do to modify the occurrence of desired outcomes. Other manifestations of control are a sense of mastery and beliefs about ways to maintain, prevent, or compensate for aging changes.

A majority of Americans believe they have control over their health. A survey conducted by *Parade* magazine and Research!America (2006) asked, "Do you think there is anything you can do to stay healthy as you grow older, or do you think the way you age is basically outside your control?" The results revealed that 84 percent of Americans believe there are things they can do to control the aging process.

It is important to make the distinction between perceptions of control and actual control. Perceived control is to some extent in the eye of the beholder. In some cases these views may be veridical; in many cases we do not really know to what extent we can control something. Nevertheless, beliefs about control do influence behavior, and the same event or situation may be seen as more or less controllable by different individuals.

With regard to aging, some believe that the associated decrements are inevitable or irreversible and others believe they are preventable or modifiable. There are interesting differences between those who believe they are in control and those who do not. A sense of control is associated with being happy, healthy, wealthy, and wise (Lachman 2006). Many studies show that those who believe aging-related outcomes are at least somewhat under their control are more likely to engage in adaptive behaviors (Lachman and Firth 2004). Certainly, there are circumstances and changes with aging that we cannot control, but when faced with such challenges, those with a higher sense of control are typically better able to cope with obstacles and losses over the long run.

The results from a large national survey (Midlife in the United States, or MIDUS; Brim, Ryff, and Kessler 2004) showed that those with a higher sense of control had a more optimistic view of adulthood. They reported that things were going well and expected circumstances to either stay that way or get even better in the future (see Lachman and Firth 2004; Lachman et al. 2008). We also have found that those with higher control are less depressed and have better self-rated health, fewer chronic conditions, and less-severe functional limitations. Sense of control also has been found to moderate the relationship between socioeconomic status (SES) and physical and mental health (Adler et al. 1994; Lachman and Weaver 1998). Among low-SES adults, those who have a high sense of control are able to maintain levels of health and well-being comparable to those with higher SES.

In the cognitive domain, sense of control is tied to better memory and greater intellectual functioning (Berry and West 1993; Grover and Hertzog 1991; Hertzog, Dixon, and Hultsch 1990; Lachman 1986, 1991; Lachman and Jelalian 1984; Stine, Lachman, and Wingfield 1993; West and Yassuda 2004). Moreover, there is evidence that those who have higher control beliefs improve more on cognitive tests with practice and are less likely to show aging-related declines in cognitive functioning over time (Caplan and Schooler 2003). Complaints about memory are common throughout adulthood (Lachman 2004), but those who have a higher sense of control are less likely to report memory problems (Lachman, Andreoletti, and Pearman 2006).

The relationship between control beliefs and aging-related outcomes, in health and cognition, is reciprocal. As Bandura's social cognitive approach (1997) suggests, expectancies for control affect outcomes, but performance/outcomes are also an important source for expectancies. Declines in health and memory, for example, may result in a lowered sense of control, in that these changes may be seen as inevitable or irreversible parts of aging. Moreover, beliefs can influence outcomes, including the maintenance of functioning, coping with losses, and prevention of further decline. Feeling a loss of control can compromise performance or health by increasing anxiety or distraction and decreasing health-promoting behaviors or other important actions.

PROTECTIVE FACTORS

In promoting healthy aging, we stress a multidisciplinary, integrative approach. It is important to consider the interrelation of biological, social, psychological, and behavioral factors (see figure 2.1). Based on an extensive review of the literature, we find a number of lifestyle factors that are associated with good health. These include factors that protect against losses and others that can compensate when losses have occurred. Cognitively stimulating activity, physical exercise, social support and engagement, stress reduction, a good education, and a high sense of control are all behavioral and psychosocial factors that can enhance health. Based on a synthesis of past studies, we present a psychosocial and behavioral prescription for aging well:

- ✦ Get a good education.
- ✦ Have a high sense of control.
- ✦ Reduce stress and anxiety.
- ✦ Exercise regularly.
- ✦ Seek out and give social support.
- ✦ Be socially engaged.
- ✦ Do cognitively stimulating activities.

The evidence suggests that it is ideal to begin these protective factors early in life and continue them throughout life, if possible. Although it is never too early to begin thinking about healthy aging, research findings show it is not too late to begin even in later life (e.g., starting to exercise in later life is still beneficial).

LIBRARIES: A FAVORABLE CONTEXT

When we think of health promotion contexts, first to come to mind are hospitals, medical clinics, health food stores, health spas, and gyms. The library is another institution that can play a central role in promoting health and well-being in adulthood. Libraries can educate people about what they can do to minimize illness and physical declines and to promote physical, cognitive, and psychological functioning. Activities can include learning for learning's sake, reading for pleasure, using a computer, looking for information about health care, attending a lecture or class, volunteering, or just being in a quiet and comfortable place with other people. Reading in its various forms, the heart of the library, is one of the activities that keep us young. Reading helps to promote better cognitive functioning, including memory, especially for those who have not had the privilege of higher education.

The library setting is conducive to many of the activities and mind-sets we presented as protective factors. For example, a library that supports lifelong learning can promote social engagement and participation in cognitively stimulating activities. Many other beneficial behaviors and habits are consistent with library policies and can be easily practiced in library settings. Many opportunities are available, but most people cannot usually take advantage of them all. This means there is a need to be flexible, to consider options, and to make choices. We can't always predict what's coming, and when obstacles arise, new paths may need to be considered.

LIBRARIES AND THE LIFE SPAN

Libraries, like people, have a life cycle, and a life-span view may be usefully applied. Library use and goals figure prominently in the lives of children, their parents, and young adults, but the library's role for the middle and later years of life still needs to be invented. Many of us remember going to the library as children. First the librarian or other adults read to us; then our parents, teachers, or older siblings checked out books for us. Getting our own library card was a major milestone. We learned how to take care of the books and return them on time. Eventually, we moved from the children's section to the adult section and used the library for schoolwork, not just for pleasure reading. As young parents, we took our own children to the library, but in middle adulthood, when the amount of leisure time declined, so did our use of the library. Missing from this life cycle conception of the library is a clearly defined role for those in later life. In many ways this undeveloped role for older adults in the library parallels their ill-defined situation in society as a whole. This is where great potential lies. The library can play a central role in finding meaningful tasks to enhance life for older adults. It is worthwhile to consider how we can use the library to enrich our lives and health throughout the life span.

It is also important to consider historical shifts and contextual factors in older adults' use of libraries. The old date stamp and ink pad are no longer the staples of a librarian's desk; a computer and bar code reader have taken their place. In the electronic age, more people may use libraries long distance through the Internet. At the same time, those who do not have access to computers and technology may be more likely to go to libraries to use these resources. The library is an ideal place to provide services for adults to increase their literacy and engagement and, hence, their health. There are, of course, many challenges. Those with low SES are more likely to have chronic conditions, which increase with age. Thus, many older adults may not be able to get to a library because of physical limitations and mobility problems. This suggests it is crucial to consider outreach methods in which the library comes to them, perhaps electronically or by conducting programs in home settings.

CONCLUSION

We can prevent, delay, reduce, or compensate for aging-related declines and losses in health. Libraries can facilitate health-promoting behaviors such as engagement in stimulating cognitive and social activities. However, those who would benefit the most are typically the least likely to participate. Nonparticipants include those who are too busy, have maladaptive/negative attitudes, or have physical disabilities and functional limitations. Thus, one major challenge is to find ways to attract those who are inactive. One possibility is distance participation. Libraries can reach out to older adults via computer, DVD, television, or radio. Another option is to take the mobile library to places where older adults live. If you can't get the older adult to the library, take the library to the older adult. The library has a promising role for health promotion and figures prominently in the behavioral prescription for living longer and living well. It makes good sense in the twenty-first century to find creative ways to link the health of the library system and the health of the populations it serves.

REFERENCES

Adler, N. E., T. Boyce, M. A. Chesney, S. Cohen, S. Folkman, R. Kahn, et al. 1994. Socioeconomic status and health: The challenge of the gradient. *American Psychologist* 49:15–24.

Baltes, P. B., U. Lindenberger, and U. M. Staudinger. 2006. Life span theory in developmental psychology. In *Handbook of child psychology: Theoretical models of human development,* ed. W. Damon and R. M. Lerner, 1:569–664. New York: Wiley.

Bandura, A. 1997. *Self-efficacy: The exercise of control.* New York: Freeman.

Berry, J. M., and R. L. West. 1993. Cognitive self-efficacy in relation to personal mastery and goal setting across the life span. *International Journal of Behavioral Development* 16:351–79.

Brim, O., C. Ryff, and R. Kessler. 2004. *How healthy are we? A national study of well-being at midlife.* Chicago: University of Chicago Press.

Caplan, L. J., and C. Schooler. 2003. The roles of fatalism, self-confidence, and intellectual resources in the disablement process in older adults. *Psychology and Aging* 18:551–61.

Cicero, M. T. 1946 [44 BC]. *De Senectute* [On old age]. Trans. William Armistead Falconer. Cambridge, MA: Harvard University Press.

Grover, D. R., and C. Hertzog. 1991. Relationships between intellectual control beliefs and psychometric intelligence in adulthood. *Journals of Gerontology: Psychological Sciences* 46B:P109–P115.

Heckhausen, J., R. A. Dixon, and P. B. Baltes. 1989. Gains and losses in development throughout adulthood as perceived by different adult age groups. *Developmental Psychology* 25:109–21.

Hertzog, C., R. A. Dixon, and D. F. Hultsch. 1990. Relationships between metamemory, memory predictions, and memory task performance in adults. *Psychology and Aging* 5:215–27.

Lachman, M. E. 1986. Locus of control in aging research: A case for multidimensional and domain-specific assessment. *Psychology and Aging* 1:34–40.

———. 1991. Perceived control over memory aging: Developmental and intervention perspectives. *Journal of Social Issues* 47:159–75.

————. 2001. *Handbook of midlife development.* New York: Wiley.

————. 2004. Development in midlife. *Annual Review of Psychology* 55:305–31.

————. 2006. Perceived control over aging-related declines: Adaptive beliefs and behaviors. *Current Directions in Psychological Science* 15:282–86.

Lachman, M. E., C. Andreoletti, and A. Pearman. 2006. Memory control beliefs: How are they related to age, strategy use and memory improvement? *Social Cognition* 24:359–85.

Lachman, M. E., and K. M. Firth. 2004. The adaptive value of feeling in control during midlife. In *How healthy are we? A national study of well-being at midlife,* ed. O. G. Brim, C. D. Ryff, and R. Kessler, 320–49. Chicago: University of Chicago Press.

Lachman, M. E., and E. Jelalian. 1984. Self-efficacy and attributions for intellectual performance in young and elderly adults. *Journal of Gerontology* 39:577–82.

Lachman, M. E., C. Röcke, C. Rosnick, and C. D. Ryff. 2008. Realism and illusion in Americans' temporal views of their life satisfaction: Age differences in reconstructing the past and anticipating the future. *Psychological Science* 19:889–97.

Lachman, M. E., and S. L. Weaver. 1998. The sense of control as a moderator of social class differences in health and well-being. *Journal of Personality and Social Psychology* 74:763–73.

Mehegan, D. 2004. Survey finds drop in reading rates. *Boston Globe,* July 9, A3.

Meyer, J. 2001. Age: 2000. U.S. Census Bureau Census 2000 brief. www.census.gov/prod/2001pubs/c2kbr01-12.pdf.

Mroczek, D. K., and A. Spiro III. 2005. Change in life satisfaction during adulthood: Findings from the Veterans Affairs Normative Aging Study. *Journal of Personality and Social Psychology* 88:189–202.

National Center for Education Statistics. 2003. National Assessment of Adult Literacy: State and county estimates of low literacy. http://nces.ed.gov/naal/estimates/overview.aspx.

National Center for Health Statistics. 2007. *Health, United States, 2007, with chartbook on trends in the health of Americans.* Washington, DC: Government Printing Office.

Pleis, J. R., and M. Lethbridge-Çejku. 2007. Summary health statistics for U.S. adults: National Health Interview Survey, 2006. National Center for Health Statistics. Vital and Health Statistics series 10, 235:1–153.

Research!America. 2006. Taking our pulse: The *Parade*/Research!America Health Poll. Alexandria, VA: Charlton Research Company. www.researchamerica.org (accessed February 20, 2009).

Rowe, J. W., and R. L. Kahn. 1998. *Successful aging.* New York: Pantheon.

Stine, E. L., M. E. Lachman, and A. Wingfield. 1993. The roles of perceived and actual control in memory for spoken language. *Educational Gerontology* 19:331–49.

Vaillant, G. E. 2002. *Aging well.* Boston: Little, Brown.

West, R. L., and M. S. Yassuda. 2004. Aging and memory control beliefs: Performance in relation to goal setting and memory self-evaluation. *Journals of Gerontology: Psychological Sciences* 59B:P56–P65.

LIBRARY LEADERSHIP FOR MATURE ADULT LEARNERS IN A CHANGING WORLD

The Importance of Attending to Developmental Diversity

Ellie Drago-Severson and Jessica Blum

With the quick-paced and ever-changing nature of contemporary living, the rapid expansion of technology, and the tumultuous, unstable economic conditions at our doorstep, twenty-first-century life is nothing if not complex. It is hardly a surprise, then, that libraries are changing markedly as well. While information technologies inarguably provide opportunities for enhanced communication, services, and resources, they simultaneously transform the familiar landscape of the traditional library in ways that require even more effective leadership and patron support (Natriello 2006). For instance, although the etymology of the word *library* primarily concerns the collection and storage of books, modern libraries offer vast collections of digital resources—and librarians function as community service providers, leaders, teachers, and technological guides as well as curators.

This transformation is particularly important given the growing number of library patrons and community citizens who face modern challenges without the luxury of a lifetime of technological learning. Currently, 20 percent of our nation is 55 or older, and by 2030, that figure is projected to grow to 30 percent (ACE 2009). Moreover, societal trends toward lifelong learning, an expanding array of post- and secondary-career options, and the changing face of retirement suggest that adults in this stage of life will seek out and be in need of information to greater degrees than ever before (see Manheimer and Kidahashi, chapter 7 in this book). From this perspective, it is clear that libraries can and do play a vital role in meeting the substantive lifelong learning needs of adults—especially those in this important age bracket, with so much wisdom to offer and so much to achieve.

In our work with adults and libraries, we have learned that there is a pressing need to better understand how to support adult learning and development. Although this, of course, is no easy task, we approach the challenge using the lens of Robert Kegan's constructive-developmental theory (1982, 1994, 2000) and Ellie Drago-Severson's pillar practices for supporting adult development (2009). We offer a new understanding of how to support adult development and practical strategies for supporting adult growth within the library context.

For example, Ellie Drago-Severson recently worked with a group of library leaders at an institute to discuss many of the ideas presented in this chapter. Janet, a library leader for over fifteen years, shared a common perspective and concern: "Collaborating with others helps me grow," she said. "Talking and thinking with others about our work—and making time for this—is what really matters. I need more knowledge about how to support adults' development in my library."

But how can we help build libraries as learning centers that support adult development? What supports do older adults—and all adults, for that matter—need to flourish? How can we support adults with different needs, preferences, and developmental orientations?

One option is to help those who serve in libraries better attend to developmental diversity. Such intentionality toward adult development—and the practices discussed herein—will help library leaders fulfill this noble goal. Accordingly we explore

1. Adult developmental theory that supports adult learning and development
2. A new model of learning-oriented leadership that can be tailored to your particular setting, including four pillar practices: teaming, providing leadership roles, engaging in collegial inquiry, and mentoring
3. Adult learning principles and why they are essential to supporting adult development

THE CONTEXT AND THE STUDY: INTERPRETING TWENTY-FIRST-CENTURY LIBRARIES AS LEARNING CENTERS

We know that when we employ practices that support adult learning, adults thrive (Drago-Severson 2004a, 2004b, 2009; Kegan 1982, 1994; Kegan and Lahey 2009; Mezirow 2000). However, we need greater knowledge about how library leaders—and all leaders, for that matter—can do this by focusing on the ways adults make sense of their experiences. The concepts discussed here are based on research conducted by Ellie Drago-Severson from 1999 to 2009, and the identified practices are those many principals employ to support adult growth and leadership. Data were gathered through qualitative interviews, surveys, and document analysis and concerned the ways principals, assistant principals, teachers, and adults in adult education programs understood effective practices used to support adult learning. The ideas and practices described in this chapter can support adults' development in libraries as well.

CONSTRUCTIVE-DEVELOPMENTAL THEORY: THE PROMISE OF ACCOMMODATING INDIVIDUAL DIFFERENCES BY ATTENDING TO DEVELOPMENTAL DIVERSITY

Robert Kegan's constructive-developmental theory (1982, 1994, 2000) illuminates how adults make meaning of their experiences in developmentally different ways and how adult growth can be supported. A "holding environment" is the context in which we grow; it can be a relationship or a series of relationships that provides developmentally appropriate supports and challenges. We define *growth* as increases in an individual's capacities (cognitive, affective, interpersonal, and intrapersonal) to better manage the demands of teaching, learning, leadership, and life. Increases in these capacities enable human beings to form broader perspectives of themselves and others.

According to Kegan (2000), the *instrumental, socializing,* and *self-authoring* ways of knowing are most common in adulthood. As a person grows toward the next way of knowing, the former becomes secondary to the new way of knowing. Much like the layering of an onion, ways of knowing overlap and change, with the primary meaning-making system outermost and prominent. However, when considering ways of knowing, it is important to remember that *development* is not the same as *intelligence;* a person can be very intelligent (i.e., high IQ) and make meaning with any one of the three ways of knowing discussed in this chapter. Moreover, each way of knowing has developmental strengths and limitations. Finally, while constructive-developmental theory is hierarchical, one way of knowing is not necessarily better than another; the fit between a person's capacities and the implicit and explicit demands of his or her environment is what is most important.

One compelling reason to attend to ways of knowing is that in any library community, adults will make sense of their experiences in developmentally different ways (Drago-Severson 2004b, 2009; Kegan 1994). Accordingly, library leaders need to attend to developmental diversity, in addition to other, more recognized forms of diversity. To do this, it is necessary to incorporate learning-oriented leadership practices in a holding environment that will support and challenge each adult (Drago-Severson 2004a, 2004b, 2009).

The Three Ways of Knowing

What is a way of knowing? A person's way of knowing is the filter through which he or she understands experiences across multiple domains (e.g., roles as workers, parents, and/or partners). It dictates and shapes beliefs about what constitutes effective help, successful practice, and the supports and challenges needed to grow.

The Instrumental Way of Knowing

An adult with an instrumental way of knowing has a "what do you have that can help me/what do I have that can help you" orientation to learning, leadership, and life. A person with this way of knowing understands that observable events have a reality separate from his or her own perspective, although the world is understood in concrete terms. Instrumental knowers tend to follow rules and feel supported when others provide specific advice and explicit procedures so that they can accomplish their work. A limitation to this way of knowing is that a person cannot take another's perspective fully. Library leaders can help instrumental knowers grow by creating safe situations to consider multiple perspectives.

The Socializing Way of Knowing

A person who uses a socializing way of knowing has an improved developmental capacity for reflection. Unlike instrumental knowers, socializing knowers have the capacity to think abstractly and to reflect on people's actions. Their orientation to the world and to their relationships is other-focused, and an adult with this way of knowing will often subordinate his or her own needs to those of others. Interpersonal conflict is almost always experienced as a threat to the self, and acceptance by authorities is of the highest importance to socializing knowers. When supporting the growth of socializing knowers, librarians can encourage and create opportunities for such knowers to voice their own opinions. Often, it is helpful to invite social-izing knowers to share their perspectives in pairs or small groups before sharing them with a larger group. This will help them clarify their own beliefs and construct their own values and standards, rather than adopting those of others. As emerging social centers for intellectual and community work (Natriello 2006), libraries offer unique opportunities for such essential dialogue and growth.

The Self-Authoring Way of Knowing

Adults with a self-authoring way of knowing generate their own internal value system, and they take ownership of their internal authority (Drago-Severson 2004b, 2006, 2009). They can identify abstract values, principles, and longer-term purposes and are able to prioritize and integrate competing values. Self-authoring knowers can assess other people's expectations and compare them to their own standards. They have the capacity to reflect on and regulate interpersonal relationships, but are limited by an inability to take perspective on their own self-authorship because they are identified with it and cannot reflect on it. Library leaders can support self-authoring knowers' growth by gently challenging them to let go of their own perspectives and embrace alternative points of view.

ATTENDING TO DEVELOPMENTAL DIFFERENCES: A DEVELOPMENTAL VIEW OF COLLABORATION

When you, as a library leader, attend to developmental differences, you can support adult development. Table 3.1 illustrates how adults with different ways of knowing will have different expectations for you as a library leader. These expectations can extend to their colleagues. A developmental mindfulness can help us to enhance libraries as genuine learning centers, facilitate constant improvement, and advance conditions for supporting adult development.

For example, many learning opportunities, such as collaboration, invite adults to share decision making. However, adults will experience this opportunity *differently* because they have different developmental capacities for generating standards, for reflecting, and for perspective taking (Drago-Severson 2004b, 2006, 2009). When supporting *instrumental* knowers, for example, clear rules for collaborative decision making would be supportive. Encouraging them to move beyond the "right" answers or the "right" goals—and toward open discussion—would help them broaden their perspectives (see table 3.2).

Adults who are *socializing* knowers look to valued colleagues or authorities (e.g., library leaders) for direction in their decision making or goal setting. They will need to be gently challenged, over time, to gradually look to themselves *first* in decision making or goal setting or both. In contrast, adults who are *self-authoring* knowers have the capacity to look internally when making decisions. While socializing knowers experience conflict with the opinions of valued colleagues or authorities as a threat to their relationships, self-authoring knowers experience conflict as a natural part of dialogue, which can lead to better solutions.

TABLE 3.1   Adults' Expectations of Supervisors: A Developmental View

WAY OF KNOWING	ADULTS' EXPECTATIONS FOR A GOOD SUPERVISOR
Instrumental Knowers	For adults who make meaning in this way, good leaders are those who show them how to learn. Effective leaders *give* instrumental knowers their knowledge and the rules they need to follow to do their work effectively. These adults know that they have performed well because they can do something (demonstrate a behavior) and because they achieve intended results.
Socializing Knowers	For these adults, effective and supportive leaders are those who care about them. Effective leaders explain things to help them understand. Good leaders really listen and offer support—effective leaders *know* what is good for these adults to know and *tell* them what they *should* know. These adults describe effective leaders as kind, patient, and encouraging. Socializing knowers can feel, inside, when they have learned something, and they value and appreciate the leader's acknowledgment.
Self-Authoring Knowers	For these adults, effective leaders are one source of knowledge, and they see themselves and peers as equally valid sources. These adults have the capacity to offer feedback to leaders to help them improve their leadership practices. They expect good leaders to listen to their feedback and to use a variety of strategies to help these adults learn and grow. Supportive leaders help self-authoring knowers meet their own internally generated goals. These adults know when they have demonstrated proficiency, and they can then think of different ways to teach what they know to others.

TABLE 3.2   Adults' Sense Making of Goal Setting: A Developmental View

WAY OF KNOWING	ADULTS' EXPECTATIONS OF LEADERS AND PEERS IN THE GOAL-SETTING PROCESS	PRACTICAL SUPPORTS
Instrumental Knowers	Leader or peer knows the *right* goals and should say what those goals are.	Give instrumental knowers specific goals and the step-by-step process for achieving them.
Socializing Knowers	Leader or peer knows the *best* goals, out of many possibilities.	Socializing knowers generate some goals internally. If these are voiced, acknowledge them as goals that *should* be pursued.
Self-Authoring Knowers	Having self-determined goals, these adults expect their leader and peers to *engage in dialogue* and to offer additional goals for consideration.	Offer feedback and critique on goals and engage in joint inquiry around the process for selecting them.

HOW LIBRARY LEADERSHIP CAN SUPPORT ADULT LEARNING: FOUR PILLAR-PRACTICES-FOR-GROWTH

The most effective holding environments provide individuals with developmentally appropriate forms of support *and* high challenge. Any one of the pillar-practices-for-growth (Drago-Severson 2004b, 2009) can serve as a "holding environment." Tables 3.3, 3.4, and 3.5 illustrate supports and challenges that will help adults with different ways of knowing to engage in these practices. Next we discuss the four *pillar practices for growth* identified to assist in supporting adult development (Drago-Severson 2004b, 2009).

TABLE 3.3   Instrumental Knowers: Supports and Challenges for Growth

SUPPORTS	CHALLENGES (GROWING EDGE)
• Setting clear goals and expectations • Providing step-by-step directions • Sharing examples of rules, purposes, and goals—and how to share them with others • Engaging in dialogue that provides concrete advice, specific skills, and information about instruction and practice	• Learning about multiple perspectives through dialogue • Creating tasks that demand abstract thinking (in the psychological sense), and scaffolding instrumental knowers through the process • Encouraging movement beyond "right" solutions and toward other perspectives • Discussing how multiple perspectives can enhance abstract thinking

Source: Table text adapted from Drago-Severson 2006.

TABLE 3.4   Socializing Knowers: Supports and Challenges for Growth

SUPPORTS	CHALLENGES (GROWING EDGE)
• Feeling known and accepted • Feeling that authorities and others confirm, acknowledge, and accept these knowers' own beliefs • Perceiving acceptance from leaders and others helps these knowers feel safe in taking risks and sharing their perspectives • Sharing perspectives in pairs or triads before sharing with larger groups • Sharing different opinions okay as long as relationships are not put in danger	• Developing *own* beliefs; becoming less dependent on others' approval • Generating *own* values and standards, not co-constructing them • Accepting conflicting points of view without feeling that they threaten relationships • Separating *own* feelings and responsibilities from another person's • Distinguishing *own* perspective from need to be accepted

Source: Table text adapted from Drago-Severson 2006.

TABLE 3.5   Self-Authoring Knowers: Supports and Challenges for Growth

SUPPORTS	CHALLENGES (GROWING EDGE)
• Learning about diverse points of view • Analyzing and critiquing ideas and exploring own goals • Learning from the *process* • Demonstrating *own* competencies • Critiquing *own* practices and contributing to developing a vision • Emphasizing competency • Inviting demonstration of competencies and dialogue	• Letting go of *own* perspective and embracing opposing alternatives • Accepting diverse problem-solving approaches that differ from own • Setting aside *own* standards for practice and opening up to other values • Accepting and learning from various ways to explore problems

Source: Table text adapted from Drago-Severson 2006.

Pillar Practice 1: Teaming

Working in teams enables adults to question their own and other people's assumptions and philosophies of teaching and learning, to evaluate curricula, to reflect on their library's mission, and to make decisions collaboratively. But voicing opinions can be perceived as risky for individuals with different ways of knowing. Instrumental knowers might need support to be able to consider multiple perspectives. Adults who are socializing knowers can find it uncomfortable initially, especially when conflict around ideas emerges. These adults need encouragement over time to understand that conflict can be a means to developing more effective solutions to dilemmas. In contrast, learning from dialogue and conflict can be stimulating to self-authoring knowers. Encouraging these adults to consider perspectives that oppose their own will support their growth. The team structure provides a safe context within which to experiment with one's thinking.

Pillar Practice 2: Providing Leadership Roles

By assuming leadership roles, adults share power and decision-making authority. A leadership role is an opportunity to raise not only one's own consciousness but also a community's consciousness. These roles enable adults to benefit from one another's expertise and knowledge. We use the term *providing leadership roles* rather than the commonly used term *distributive leadership* because of the intention behind these roles. Rather than assigning tasks, providing leadership roles offers supports and challenges to the adult so he or she can develop.

Working with others invites adults to share authority and ideas as they work toward building their library communities, reaching individual life goals, and promoting change. Leadership roles can help adults negotiate the often competing demands of providing and receiving support, while attending to their own practice and larger societal needs. Engaging in leadership roles and supporting other adults in these roles create opportunities to tailor support and challenge to individual needs.

As with teaming, leadership roles can be perceived differently by adults. While those who are challenged by assuming their own authority (instrumental and socializing knowers) might initially require considerable support as they take on leadership, self-authoring knowers might appreciate the opportunity to put their ideas into action. Leadership roles can serve as effective holding environments, especially when supports and challenges are offered to the person assuming the role. This way, the experience can be used not simply as an additional responsibility but as an opportunity for growth.

Pillar Practice 3: Engaging in Collegial Inquiry

Collegial inquiry (CI) is a type of reflective practice that can occur individually or in groups. It is a dialogue that involves purposefully reflecting on one's assumptions as part of the learning process. CI provides opportunities to develop more complex perspectives by listening to others. Adults in Drago-Severson's research used CI to engage with other adults in decision making and learning about key issues (e.g., diversity, proposals for change). Examples include

- ✦ reflecting privately in writing in response to probing questions or sentence stems, followed by discussion
- ✦ engaging in the process of collaborative goal setting with others
- ✦ reflecting collectively as a method of engaging in conflict resolution

As adults—especially those at transitional life stages—consider, investigate, and explore future paths, opportunities for group reflection and assumption recognition can be effective and growth-promoting holding environments.

Pillar Practice 4: Mentoring

Mentoring traditionally offers a more private, yet relational, way of supporting adult development. This practice creates an opportunity for broadening perspectives, examining assumptions, and sharing expertise. It takes many forms, including pairing adults with other adults who have particular areas of expertise, pairing adults who have deep knowledge of a library's mission with other adults new to a library community, and group or team mentoring.

As you may already suspect, our ways of knowing will indeed influence what we expect of and need from mentors. They also influence the kinds of supports and challenges that help us grow. For example, instrumental knowers will feel supported by mentors who help them meet concrete needs and goals. Mentors who explain the step-by-step procedures for achieving their concrete goals will support these adults. Over time, however, a mentor can support growth by encouraging a mentee to move beyond the perceived *right* goals or *right* way of doing things. Ultimately, more open-ended discussions about alternatives and abstract goals can help broaden the mentee's perspective and thinking.

A socializing knower will feel supported by a mentor's explicit acknowledgment of the importance of the knower's beliefs and ideas. Feeling accepted and cared for—as a person—by mentors will enable these adults to take greater learning risks. Mentors can gently support these mentees' growth by encouraging them to *voice* their own perspectives *before* learning about those of others. In addition, modeling that conflict can be helpful without threatening the relationship will support growth.

Self-authoring knowers will feel best supported by mentors who enable them to learn about diverse perspectives and to critique and analyze their own *and their mentor's* perspectives, goals, and practices. To support growth, mentors can encourage these adults to move away from their investments in their own philosophy without feeling internally conflicted (Drago-Severson 2009).

In summary, the way in which we, as adults, engage in the pillar practices or any form of learning and collaborative work (i.e., shared decision making) varies according to *how* we make sense of our experiences. With appropriate supports and challenges, though, we can grow and participate in these processes and in society even more effectively. We hope the pillar practices offer assistance as we work to build libraries to be robust learning centers.

IMPLICATIONS: CONSIDERING DEVELOPMENTAL DIVERSITY WHEN SUPPORTING MATURE ADULT LEARNERS

This chapter advocates a way of enhancing conditions for building libraries as learning centers through *learning-oriented leadership.* By drawing on current research and constructive-developmental theory, the chapter offers specific practices supportive of adults' development (Drago-Severson 2004b, 2009). Indeed, in our fast-paced society, the need *to know* is—in many ways and for many people—as fundamental a requirement as our basic safety and belongingness needs (Ansello 1982). As adults 55 and over work to make sense of their options, opportunities, and future directions, libraries will necessarily play key roles for continuing learners. The learning-oriented leadership practices described in this chapter can help library leaders better facilitate this important transition and can help adults develop capacities to better manage the complexities of living and learning in the twenty-first century. It is important to note also that although the developmental orientations described in this chapter apply to the majority of *all* adults, the pillar practices will prove effective when considering how *older* adults make meaning of their experiences and what kinds of information and support they require along the way.

The four pillar practices that comprise this model can assist you, as library leader, as you work to build relationships, strengthen collaboration, and support your own and others' development. This work holds four key implications:

1. Library leaders can benefit from a developmental perspective because adults will experience information-seeking, community-building, and learning opportunities in different ways.
2. A developmental vocabulary helps us move away from labeling adults based on behaviors.
3. Older adults, like younger adults, need different supports and challenges, which can be embedded in the four pillar practices to support their development.
4. Consideration of the developmental match between the expectations of a culture, the pressures of a life stage or transition, and adults' capacities to meet those expectations and pressures will help shape libraries as learning centers that support adult development.

Understanding the three most common ways of knowing and the pillar practices can help library leaders offer older adults appropriate supports and challenges as they explore the multiplicity of emerging opportunities for personal growth, collaboration, new learning, and community impact. (For more on these practices, see Drago-Severson 2004b, 2009.) As social and knowledge centers for individual, intellectual, and community work, libraries—and those who lead them—can provide the scaffolding necessary to effectively support older adult patrons. We hope that the practices and ideas presented in this chapter will help you in your efforts to support the learning, growth, and dreams of others.

REFERENCES

ACE American Council on Education. 2009. *Reinvesting in the third age.* www.acenet.edu/Content/NavigationMenu/ProgramsServices/CLLL/Reinvesting/index.htm.

Ansello, E. F. 1982. Mature adult learners and the need to know. *Contemporary Educational Psychology* 7 (2): 139–51.

Drago-Severson, E. 2004a. *Becoming adult learners: Principles and practices for effective development.* New York: Teachers College Press.

———. 2004b. *Helping teachers learn: Principal leadership for adult growth and development.* Thousand Oaks, CA: Corwin Press.

———. 2006. How can you better support teachers' growth? *The Learning Principal* 1 (6): 1, 6–7. Oxford, OH: National Staff Development Council.

———. 2009. *Leading adult learning: Supporting adult development in our schools.* Thousand Oaks, CA: Corwin Press/Sage.

Kegan, R. 1982. *The evolving self: Problems and process in human development.* Cambridge, MA: Harvard University Press.

———. 1994. *In over our heads: The mental demands of modern life.* Cambridge, MA: Harvard University Press.

———. 2000. What "form" transforms? A constructive-developmental approach to transformative learning. In *Learning as transformation,* ed. J. Mezirow and Associates, 35–70. San Francisco: Jossey-Bass.

Kegan, R., and L. L. Lahey. 2009. *Immunity to change: How to overcome it and unlock the potential in yourself and your organization.* Boston: Harvard Business School Press.

Mezirow, J. 2000. Learning to think like an adult: Core concepts of transformation theory. In *Learning as transformation: Critical perspectives on a theory in progress,* ed. J. Mezirow, 3–33. San Francisco: Jossey-Bass.

Natriello, G. 2006. Seminar on the future of libraries: Progress report. Working Paper Publication. EdLab at Teachers College, Columbia University. http://edlab.tc.columbia.edu/index.php?q=node/512.

THE IMPORTANCE OF SPIRITUALITY IN AN AGING SOCIETY | 4

Robert C. Atchley

WHAT IS SPIRITUALITY?

As it is used today, the term *spirituality* refers to an inner, subjective aspect of life that revolves around individual experiences of *being, transcending* the personal self, and *connecting* with the sacred. Conceptions of the sacred range from non-deistic ideas such as the Buddhist Void to the "God beyond God" of Meister Eckhart and Paul Tillich to personified conceptions of God in Judaism, Christianity, and Islam to conceptions of the sacred as residing in nature. The latter perspective is a major element of Native American as well as Celtic spirituality. As a subjective experience, spirituality involves developing the capacity to perceive and organize occurrences of intangible spiritual elements of existence. For example, whether people experience wonder upon seeing Niagara Falls or the Grand Canyon depends to some extent on how open they are to this experience within themselves. Wonder is not inherent in the falls or the canyon but is a response to these places by an individual human being.

Experiences labeled spiritual by my interview respondents are described in terms of specific qualities, such as wonder, compassion, clarity, stillness, silence, or expansiveness. Most spiritual experiences have only one or two of these spiritual qualities. Spiritual experiences can occur through various avenues, such as the senses, consciousness/awareness, thought, or transcendence. Spiritual practices are activities designed in part to cultivate and develop these various avenues of spiritual experience. (For more detail on these concepts, see Atchley 2009.)

Part of spiritual experience involves perception of intangible or ineffable aspects of stimuli. Another part involves the developed capacities of the perceiver—for experiencing pure being, for experiencing a level of awareness that dispassionately witnesses the "I" who acts, and for experiencing a connection with a being or web of being far greater than individual existence.

Having spiritual experiences motivates most people to want more spiritual experiences because of the qualities associated with spiritual experience. Of course, to perceive and categorize experiences as spiritual requires having concepts and language concerning what spirituality is. Historically, people got the needed vocabulary from religious cultures. But particularly since 1970 a separate nonreligious vocabulary of spirituality has emerged and is being used by people both within and outside religious contexts (Atchley 2009; Roof 1999; Wilber 2006; Wuthnow 1998). As people develop their capacities for spiritual experience, they also usually develop their capacity for understanding a bigger range of their experiences as fitting into a meaningful spiritual context.

Some people develop their spiritual capacities spontaneously and nonconsciously. But many people engage in a conscious and deliberate effort to nurture and develop these capabilities. One way that spiritual experiences add to meaning is through contemplation of one's individual spiritual journey. Another is by conscious efforts to grow spiritually by engaging in spiritual inquiry, practice, and contemplation. Most people prefer to be accompanied on the spiritual journey by a network of supportive friends and family. Most also participate in a spiritual community, a group organized around spiritual aims and often for religious purposes.

Most people can answer the question "Do you see yourself as being on a spiritual journey?" And most who do see themselves this way can give a brief summary. They can do this because they have given a good deal of contemplative, introspective thought to their history of spiritual experiences, the spiritual integration they experience at the moment, their network of spiritual friends, and their sense of spiritual direction.

Spiritual journeys are histories of the experiences, actions, and insights connected with a quest for spiritual meaning. The story of a person's spiritual journey weaves together themes and events over time and usually includes both ups and downs. Spiritual journeys tell us how people became the spiritual beings they are now, the processes they went through, and sometimes where the person sees her or his journey leading. Spiritual journeys of older people usually include an element of learning to persist and be content on a journey into imperfectly known territory, where insights are usually limited, no matter how profound they may seem at the time. These journeys are often described with humor in the face of life's contradictions and paradoxes, which are themselves food for contemplation. There is often a "let be" attitude toward "progress" on the journey, an understanding that development cannot be forced. There is much wisdom in elders' spoken or written spiritual journeys, not wisdom as something one might claim or make into adages, but wisdom as a living process we each can aspire to. Each of the hundreds of spiritual journeys I have listened to or read is a unique expression of the person telling the story.[1] Opportunities to tell these stories are still in short supply, even in most spiritual communities, yet where such opportunities routinely exist they are usually very well attended.

Personal narratives about spiritual journeys capture an important element of integration in the lives of most aging people, yet there has been very little analytical study of these accounts to discover what we can learn from them. In particular, how do spiritual journeys relate to other personal narratives and how do spiritual journeys relate to life decisions? What difference does it make when the spiritual journey becomes a master narrative?

Many aging people engage in conscious efforts to nurture their spiritual capacities. They can do this through having an enduring set of questions used to remain spiritually self-aware; being committed to regular spiritual practices (such as contemplative reading, meditation, or prayer) or movement practices (such as yoga or labyrinth walking); participating in a spiritual community; participating in workshops or retreats aimed at spiritual growth; or participating in peer-support groups aimed at providing social support for the spiritual journey and opportunities for expression.

A large proportion of aging and older people find their voice concerning spirituality through the language of their religion. Others see spirituality as separate from religion.[2] It is very important that we not impose one view or the other. Wuthnow (1998) and Roof (1999) agree that generations born before World War II tend to see religion and spirituality as two sides of the same coin. However, those born in the late 1940s and after tend to separate the two. They see religion primarily as the history, organizational structure, and culture of a religious denomination or subgroup, and they see spirituality as an internal realm over which the individual is the ultimate authority in terms of how to perceive, strive for, organize, and integrate spiritual experiences. These more recent generations tend to see the spiritual journey as their personal responsibility, brought to life through choices they make and attention to life experiences following from those choices.

SPIRITUALITY AND MEANING

The question of meaning addresses basic needs for sense (understanding how things happen and why), significance (the order of things in a system of values), and purpose (having a clear set of goals).

Spiritual development leads to nonpersonal, self-transcendent awareness, which can in turn lead to a deeper sense of meaning and understanding. From this vantage point, life may make more sense.

People who experience the intensity of pure present-moment awareness are drawn toward opportunities to experience this intensity again. People who experience the clarity of perception and purpose that can come with the experience of transcending the personal self are attracted to practices that make such transcending more likely. People who experience a direct connection with the sacred, however briefly, tend to want to integrate that experience into all regions of life. These experiences dramatically increase the significance of spirituality for self-perception and as a context for life decisions.

People who have spiritual experiences, particularly if they have experiences at all three levels—being, self-transcendence, and connection with the sacred—tend to place spirituality in the top category of their hierarchy of values. Having spiritual experiences also usually expands the context or mental space within which individuals attribute meaning to various life experiences, including spiritual ones.

Spiritual development expands the context within which sense, significance, and purpose are arrived at. The notion of spiritual growth and development accurately conveys the prospect that the spiritual context can continue to expand throughout a lifetime.

SPIRITUALITY AND THE EXPERIENCE OF AGING

Continuing to develop spiritually is important to most aging people. Bringing spirituality increasingly and more unobtrusively to bear in social relationships is also important. Spirituality can be an important coping strategy in dealing with the challenges of aging. Expectations about spirituality in later life can also be a source of discomfort or distress. The experience of aging creates new opportunities for spiritual growth.

Continuing to grow spiritually is an important frontier for most aging people. The theory of gerotranscendence (Tornstam 2005) asserts that spiritual development gradually and steadily increases from middle age on and results in a shift from a materialistic, role-oriented life philosophy to a transcendent, spiritual perspective in late old age. Gerotranscendence is present to some extent in most aging adults, according to the theory, but becomes a prevalent perspective mainly in adults over 70. Gerotranscendence theory presumes that spiritual development is intrinsic and that the exact source of this development is unspecified. Nevertheless, this development can be promoted or stifled by social factors such as language and normative constraints, opportunity structures, social class, and education. Thus, the degree of gerotranscendence varies even within the very old population.

The broadened spiritual perspective that typifies mature gerotranscendence is indicated by three dimensions. In the *cosmic* dimension, concepts such as life, death, space, and time are seen as involving an element of mystery and are seen against a backdrop of infinity. In the *self-transcendent* dimension, the personal self is no longer the center of attention, and there is increased honesty about and acceptance of the personal self. In the *social selectivity* dimension, relationships focus mainly on close friends and family, and much less energy is spent on relating to casual acquaintances and strangers, with a consequent welcome increase in solitude and less emphasis on pro forma role playing. Attitudes toward material possessions shift from acquisition to maintaining the bare essentials for a comfortable life. Social selectivity leads to a much more thoughtful, contemplative stance toward relationships, activities, and lifestyles. Gerotranscendence results in less concern with social conformity for conformity's sake.

Historically, the role of elder in the community was assumed to have a spiritual element. Elders were seen not only as keepers of spiritual traditions but also as human beings who had benefited from decades of spiritual development. Although most communities no longer assume that spiritual development is connected with lengthy life experience and do not ascribe the role of elder to all older people, important vestiges of the functional role of spiritual elders remain, especially in families but also in friendship networks and in spiritual communities.

Sages are people who can manifest wisdom and retain a strong spiritual connection in the face of life's trials. In the stages and processes through which aging people develop into sages, we get a glimmer of the internal processes that complement the theory of gerotranscendence (Atchley 2003). We have learned a lot in recent years about practices that increase people's chances of developing the spiritual vantage points from which they can experience gerotranscendence and manifest in the world as sages. At all levels of human organization, we need wisdom, but who are the wisdom keepers? Where do we look? Wisdom does not reside in our libraries or in our university curriculums or on the Internet, although the arcane markings of wisdom can be found in these places. Wisdom is a human capacity that can only be fully manifested by individual human beings. Circles of at least three sages are especially capable of seeing the wisdom needed in specific situations. Most people with the capacity to be wise are older people, and unfortunately in our culture we seldom ask older people to be wise for us. Nevertheless, sages continue to quietly and unobtrusively bring wisdom to bear on human concerns in a wide variety of relationships.

Sages connect with others primarily as mentors and compassionate listeners, but their very presence in a group can also invoke a sense of greater space and luminosity. Sages are not rare, but we have to pay close attention to see them. (For more on sages, see Atchley 2009.)

Having a positive outlook is a primary strategy for coping with the challenges and opportunities of aging. Spiritual development, especially developing the capacity for being in the present, transcending the personal self, and connecting with the sacred, is a foundation of positive outlook for a large proportion of elders. In my twenty-year longitudinal study of adaptation in aging (Atchley 1999), I was astounded at the deep peace and equanimity with which many people grappled with serious disabilities and chronic illnesses, including dementia. People use their spiritual orientation in coping for at least two reasons. First, spiritual orientation is an important part of worldview. It is a way of making sense out of what is happening. Second, the cumulative results of having taken a transcendent view of the world in many situations over many years can create ease in taking that viewpoint when difficult challenges arise in the present (Atchley 2006).

Spiritual orientation can be an important part of coping, but it is not the only effective strategy. Many people who do not see themselves as spiritual nevertheless have strengths they can use to cope. Spiritual coping with aging seems to work best for people who have been using this strategy for many years.

Expectations spur much excellence, but they also cause much suffering. To the extent that individuals focus on spiritual experiences and the development of a broader context in which to place those experiences, they are less likely to be fixated on particular social or personal outcomes and are more likely to be open to dealing forthrightly with what happens, however unpleasant. The more rigid and intricate a person's expectations are concerning the link between spiritual beliefs and specific outcomes, the greater the potential for suffering and disillusionment.

CONCLUSION

People who see themselves as having spiritual experiences, as being spiritual persons on a spiritual journey, and as having experienced direct connection with the sacred are qualitatively different from people who see nothing spiritual in their lives. How people answer the question "What is life about?" matters very much for how they experience aging and how aging affects their experience. Compared with people who do not cultivate their inner life, people who pay more attention to their inner life as they age tend to have less fear of death, experience less stress, and have a more positive attitude in the face of difficulties such as chronic illness, disability, or bereavement. Thus, how a person experiences aging can be influenced substantially by the presence of a spiritual viewpoint, its content, and the degree to which that viewpoint has developed. For a sizable majority of adults entering the aging population over the next twenty years, spirituality is very relevant to their adaptation and life satisfaction. For about a third, the spiritual life is a master narrative that greatly influences choices of lifestyles, activities, webs of friendship, and communities of service. Most people are active participants in their own spiritual development, and they make wide use of books, articles, workshops, study groups, and service opportunities that they see as supporting their spiritual journeys. They tend to be seekers of a very positive sort.

NOTES

1. Since 1995, I have interviewed more than seventy-five people in depth about their spiritual journeys. I have listened to dozens of participants in spiritual support groups talk about their spiritual journeys, and I have attended more than a hundred formal presentations of spiritual journeys made by middle-aged and older adults. In addition, I have read several spiritual autobiographies and briefer accounts of spiritual journeys published in books and in journals.

2. The conceptual and linguistic relation between spirituality and religion is in the mind of the beholder, so it is unsurprising that there are many views on this subject. Some see religion as the master concept, with "religiousness" as the subjective element, which may include spirituality. Others use *spirituality* as the more general term for subjective experiences of certain types and see religiously related experiences as a subtype. These are not trivial differences. They go to the heart of conceptual meaning. There are experiences people categorize as spiritual that have for them no connection with religion as they understand that term. It seems therefore inaccurate to subsume this experience under religion. Also, if we use borrowed religious language to speak about spirituality, it is very difficult to avoid bringing along the theological elements of that language, in which case we impose a theological overlay on conversations about spirituality. This is a profound problem for most existing measures of spirituality and leads to alienation and nonresponse in potential research participants who do not share the theological overlay. I believe that a nonreligious language of spirituality developed in our culture precisely to deal with the problem of exclusion and that we should use this more inclusive language to communicate about spirituality as a subject in its own right. Spirituality and religion are inextricably interrelated for most people, but we should not use this fact to justify ignoring the perspectives of those for whom such a connection is not true.

REFERENCES

Atchley, R. C. 1999. *Continuity and adaptation in aging.* Baltimore: Johns Hopkins University Press.

———. 2003. Becoming a spiritual elder. In *Aging, spirituality, and religion: A handbook,* ed. M. A. Kimble and S. H. McFadden, 2:33–46. Minneapolis: Fortress Press.

———. 2006. Continuity, spiritual growth, and coping in later adulthood. *Journal of Religion, Spirituality, and Aging* 18 (2/3): 19–29.

———. 2009. *Spirituality and aging.* Baltimore: Johns Hopkins University Press.

Roof, C. W. 1999. *The spiritual marketplace: Baby boomers and the remaking of American religion.* Princeton, NJ: Princeton University Press.

Tornstam, L. 2005. *Gerotranscendence: A developmental theory of positive aging.* New York: Springer.

Wilber, Ken. 2006. *Integral spirituality.* Boston: Integral Books.

Wuthnow, R. 1998. *After heaven: Spirituality in America since the 1950s.* Berkeley: University of California Press.

WORK AND PURPOSE AFTER 50

5

Stephen Ristau

THE MEANING OF WORK

Work has long captured the attention of theorists, poets, and writers. The language used to define it ranges from the concrete (manual labor, toil, and trade) to the pragmatic (employment, occupation, and business) to the ethereal (calling, métier, and vocation).

Austrian psychoanalyst Sigmund Freud wrote: "The communal life of human beings had . . . a two-fold foundation: the compulsion to work, which was created by external necessity, and the power of love" (2005, 88).

Khalil Gibran, the Lebanese-American artist, poet, and philosopher, said, "When you work you fulfill a part of earth's furthest dream, assigned to you when that dream was born" (1923, 13). He continued,

And I say that life is indeed darkness save when there is urge,
And all urge is blind save when there is knowledge.
And all knowledge is vain save when there is work,
And all work is empty save when there is love;
And when you work with love you bind yourself to yourself,
and to one another, and to God.
. . .
Work is love made visible. (1923, 14)

And the American oral historian, actor, and broadcaster Studs Terkel said, "I want, of course, peace, grace, and beauty. How do you do that? You work for it. . . . And this is my belief, too: that it's the community in action that accomplishes more than any individual does, no matter how strong he may be" (2005).

THE LANGUAGE OF AGING

As with work, much has been proffered about human aging across the life span. Definitions abound as to what constitutes an "old" age, even more so today in light of the thirty-year gain in longevity since the beginning of the twentieth century. Marc Freedman, founder of Civic Ventures and author of two groundbreaking books (*Prime Time: How Baby Boomers Will Revolutionize Retirement and Transform America* and *Encore*), notes that these thirty years are added to the middle of life, resulting in new opportunities for healthy, productive, and engaged living (1999; 2007).

The baby boom generation, as well chronicled as any generation of Americans, represents a cohort of 78 million born between the years 1946 and 1964. With the leading-edge boomers now approaching what has been familiarly known as the retirement years, Freedman and others posit that whether due to economic necessity, the desire to apply one's accumulated skills and experience, or the drive to make a difference in one's community, this stage of extended middle age will redefine work and retirement, not to mention the very process of aging itself.

Moreover, with those people now 90–94 years of age representing the fastest-growing segment of our population, we can expect three generations of people 50 years old and older living at the same time. Depending on one's perspective, this situation can present grave challenges as three generations of older Americans vie for limited resources, or it can offer opportunities for new forms of intergenerational living and community building.

The phenomenon of multiple adult cohorts living simultaneously also reveals the limitations of the language we use to describe this second half of life. The brave new world of aging compels us to make sense of out-of-date terminology such as *old age, senior citizen, elders* and *elderly,* and, yes, even *retirees.* New relativistic language that proclaims "70 is the new 50" and other marketing gimmicks and imagery that promote lifetime youthfulness will capture the value and fullness of life in the second half.

CHANGE AND LONGEVITY

The world that the boomer generation has grown up in has transformed in dramatic ways. No previous generation has contributed to and experienced such profound and accelerated change in their lifetimes. Leading-edge boomers especially (those born between 1946 and 1955) have directly influenced sociopolitical and economic movements, including issues of civil rights, war and peace, women's rights, environmental stewardship, sexuality and sexual orientation, and global economies, not to mention the technology boom.

With advances in health information and medical care, boomers can expect to live longer, healthier, and more productive lives. With these bonus years of good health, many social scientists predict that boomers will redefine how older adults will face aging, retirement, work, learning, leisure, and volunteerism.

In *Re-Visioning Retirement,* a pioneering, comprehensive study of what retirement is today—and what it is transforming into—author and gerontologist Ken Dychtwald (2002) reported that the majority of retirees and pre-retirees do not regard retirement as an extended vacation or a time of rest and relaxation. And rather than seeking retirement "security," new generations are in search of a new vision of retirement "freedom."

Whether these new opportunities for choice and creative invention of new roles in the second half of life are truly an option or a limitation caused by turbulent economic conditions is a matter of great debate. So, too, are the questions of whether the current downturn is unlike any other the boomer generation has faced, and whether without an economic rebound any of the aforementioned options will be available.

To become absorbed in this debate, however, risks overlooking important trends and characteristics about boomers, longevity, and work. A long-term and significant body of research concludes that American boomers anticipate working in their retirement years whether they have to or not (AARP/Roper ASW 2001; Anthony 2001; Greller and Dee 1989; Retirement Reality Check 2002; Savishinsky 2000). The questions are "How?" and "Under what terms and conditions?"

Often understated are the changes in the workplace realities that boomers have experienced for much of their work lives. Plant closings and corporate "rightsizings" represent a highly volatile and uncertain marketplace where job security and company loyalty, the foundations of the traditional employment compact, are no longer certain. On top of that, for some boomers, there exists a growing disconnect between the goals of employers and the values of employees. Bill McKendree, president of the Clarion Group, a leading U.S. organization consulting firm, refers to this phenomenon as the *container effect*. He writes, "The long-standing corporate quest for profits and shareholder return has been overshadowed by an upwelling cry for greater purpose. Many executives and employees now find themselves questioning whether what is right for their company is right for them" (2001). McKendree adds that when business goals such as profit, speed, growth, efficiency, customer service, and shareholder return are accepted as values and guiding principles, a fundamental disconnect begins to develop between what employees know intuitively and what they want to believe for the sake of the company.

Interspersed with themes of *giving back, making a difference, freedom and choice,* and *purposeful relationships* are boomers' real economic security concerns and their desire to use skills and talents honed by a lifetime of experience.

For twenty years or more, adult boomers have developed effective "work-family balance" and "re-careering" strategies, adapting to changing personal and family needs over the life span and across unpredictable business trends. As a generation, they have changed jobs, even careers, more than any other generation in history. They are likely to push upward the average age and the sheer numbers of older Americans in the workforce to levels never seen before. Boomers are the pioneers ushering in a new era of cyclic careers over the life span (Dychtwald 2003).

It is clear that the boomers' drive to work is influenced by a number of factors, including the need for income, for self-esteem, for a sense of achievement or contribution, for social connection, for meaning and passion, and for fun. Above all, experts who have studied this transition seem to agree with the conclusions of Joel Savishinsky's research: "What many emphasized was the element of control—that retirement had given them the freedom *to* work, but at their discretion, rather than the freedom *from* working in an absolute sense. Work had become more of a choice and pleasure than a duty" (2000, 147).

WORK AND PURPOSE

The notion of purposeful work—that is, utilizing one's skills and experience to make a difference in the lives of others—has become increasingly attractive for people of all ages but for boomers in particular. Developmental psychologist Erik Erikson posited that the virtues of generativity and ego integrity are the opportunities of middle to later adulthood. Generativity, the psychological drive to care for the generations that follow oneself and often instigated by one's growing awareness of one's mortality, motivates boomers to examine their life's body of work and (re)commit to serving others and community in their time that remains. Ego integrity or wisdom is achieved in the final stage of one's life when one is able to evaluate the totality of that lifetime, feel fulfilled, and have a sense of unity within oneself and with others (Erikson 1959).

> "Baby boomers have always been in the how-do-I-find-meaning business," says Howard Husock, who directs the Manhattan Institute's Social Entrepreneurship Initiative, which honors innovative charitable actions annually. Now, he says, with many reaching retirement age and expecting to live another twenty or thirty years, "they have the luxury of being able to reflect on what meaning is and act on it." (Kadlec 2007)

In the Career Transition Study conducted in 2003 in the metro Hartford, Connecticut, region, I examined whether the increasing sense of purpose or contribution to improve the lives of others was a driving factor in the work lives of boomers as well as whether nonprofit and public service organizations were aware of and ready to tap into this talent and passion (Ristau and Leadership Greater Hartford 2003). Work was defined as encompassing the spectrum of paid and unpaid (volunteer or pro bono) engagements, full time or episodic.

My findings are corroborated by more recent national studies convened by the National Council on Aging (2008), the Conference Board (Casner-Lotto 2007), and AARP (2005), which conclude that opportunities for work with meaning and purpose for boomers are possible and even probable. Here are some key findings:

A unique opportunity exists to utilize the talents, experience, and motivation of older adults at midcourse in meaningful work in the nonprofit and public service sectors. Overwhelmingly, baby boomers and nonprofit leaders see this potential.

The search for meaning and purpose drives many boomers to the mission-related work of nonprofit and public service organizations. Although many nonprofits either are not ready to engage the talents and passion of older adults or question the sustained commitment of boomers to their mission, there seems to be fertile ground to explore the mutual benefits that greater linkages between these two groups could bring.

Leading motivators for boomers in work transition are *helping others, making a difference, using their skills,* and *finding meaningful work.* Boomers want to have an impact, be respected and appreciated, and make social connections. They are attracted to flexible work schedules and the availability of health care benefits. Earning an income or leaving stressful working conditions in another sector are at the bottom of the list of motivating drivers reported.

Although compensation and other financial benefits are not among the top drivers cited by boomer pre-retirees regarding work in retirement, the Career

Transition Study (Ristau and Leadership Greater Hartford 2003) and national surveys (Moen 1998) confirm that for economic and cultural reasons, many boomers expect to continue working for some level of pay. As Moen (1998) notes, for most adults, paid work is a major, if not the principal, source of purposeful activity, social relations, independence, identity, and self-respect. New models of volunteer or pro bono contributions are attractive to boomers as options along a work continuum of paid employment and fee-based and unpaid opportunities.

Boomers in transition report having the greatest interest in working in human and social services, education, faith-based initiatives, leadership development, and health services. Interestingly, nursing and other health professions, education, and social services are the leading occupations with projected workforce shortages in the coming decade.

Nonprofit organization leaders, while acknowledging this opportunity, are not prepared to capitalize on it and need help both conceptually and operationally. Many nonprofit leaders indicate that it would be useful to have a dedicated resource to help broker or match boomer talent with community needs as well as to assist them in developing alternative workforce strategies.

Training, orientation, and introductory internships might help create the necessary bridges for older adults in transition from private- and public-sector careers to the nonprofit sector. Common myths and stereotypes about all sectors sometimes present barriers to purposeful and productive relationships.

There is a paucity of community resources designed to assist individuals in midcourse transition to examine their assets, interests, and goals and to explore the opportunities for contribution, especially in the nonprofit sector. Few organizations provide the kind of hands-on bridge work required to prepare highly experienced older adults and nonprofit organizations for mutually purposeful relationships. Current volunteer matching programs are undercapitalized and too limited in scope to address this opportunity adequately.

Local resources that target baby boomers in transition have an expanding potential of addressing critical community issues. Such resources can also help people who are approaching the traditional retirement years with different needs and expectations but without a pathway to navigate this new life stage. New partnerships among the for-profit, nonprofit, and public sectors are possible.

All these factors mean that the time is ripe for innovation—on both individual and organizational levels. This is a social movement that merges mission and market, purpose and profits, significance and success and is doing so through radically different methods and structures. It is spawning new thinking, new concepts, and new language as it defines itself. Terms like *midcareer transitioners, re-careering, encore careers, pro bono consultants, bridgers,* and *sector switchers* and discussions about multigenerational workforces and flexible workplaces, compensation options, and hours are part of the new vocabulary of work (Ristau 2008).

LIBRARIES AND INNOVATION

A recent surge in research and development investments and activities has stimulated the early stages of transformation in the ways public libraries serve and engage baby boomers in their communities. Recognizing that the prevailing library models of serving older adults do not match the psycho-demography of the boomer cohort, a web of committed national and regional philanthropic, professional, nonprofit, and public-sector institutions have done groundbreaking work in building a more relevant and effective public library system for boomers.

Collectively, these innovative initiatives have helped to position public libraries as catalysts, resources, meeting places, and partners in creating opportunities for boomers to teach and learn, to build new skills to re-career, and to become civically active. These initiatives assert that if boomers can be effectively mobilized and engaged, they will become a social resource of unprecedented proportions by actively participating in the life of their communities—and in public libraries—contributing their time, skills, passion, and financial resources to create a social legacy of profound importance.

As stewards of reliable information and lifelong learning, public libraries are ideally positioned to become cornerstone institutions for boomers and productive aging. Some examples of leading-edge library organizational and program development follow:

> With the leadership and support of the Virginia G. Piper Charitable Trust (www.pipertrust.org/initiatives/nextchapter.aspx), the Maricopa County, Arizona (greater Phoenix), region has been an incubator of innovation and promising practices related to boomers and retirees. The Piper Trust has invested in four Next Chapter initiatives, two of which prominently involve public libraries. Located in the Tempe Public Library, Tempe Connections offers a café with rich educational, life planning, re-careering, volunteer, and arts and cultural programs (www.tempeconnections.org). In Chandler, the public library is home to Boomerang, a collaboration of community institutions and resources that serves boomers with financial, career, volunteer, and enrichment programs (www.myboomerang.org).

> In Newton, Massachusetts, a grassroots group of committed residents has partnered with the Newton Public Library to create Discovering What's Next: Revitalizing Retirement, a program to inform, inspire, and involve boomers and retirees (www.discoveringwhatsnext.com). And in Portland, Oregon, the Multnomah County Public Library is a core partner in Life By Design NW, a collaboration funded primarily by the Atlantic Philanthropies to assist boomers to discover, design, and engage with what's next in their lives (www.lifebydesignnw.org).

> The California State Library has launched a multiyear statewide initiative, Transforming Life After 50: Public Libraries and Baby Boomers, to promote learning, capacity building, and community impact (http://transforminglifeafter50.org). To date, forty-five library systems have participated, with three-quarters completing community assessment and planning projects. Recently,

twenty-four public libraries received innovation grants to support new local initiatives targeting boomers, the results of which will be disseminated and discussed in a series of symposia for other library leaders in 2009–2010 and will be part of a new dedicated website. One by-product of this project is Get Involved: Powered By Your Library, a strategic approach to position libraries in California as centers for civic engagement. The program features a partnership with VolunteerMatch, the leading online volunteer recruitment resource, to expand the engagement of skilled volunteers of all ages, especially boomers and retirees (www.library.ca.gov/lds/getinvolved.html).

Opportunities to serve and engage boomers through libraries and their community partners abound, and a growing body of innovative structures, competencies, and practices is forming. But challenges exist institutionally and professionally. As public libraries have adapted to the unique needs and assets of children, teens, and seniors, so too must they retool for the boomers in their communities.

How can libraries contribute to enriching the lives of baby boomers in their communities? What information resources, programs, and tools, both new and rebranded, can they provide that promote healthy aging, civic engagement, lifelong learning, encore careers and new ways to work, creativity, and growth throughout the life span? How will library professionals acquire the knowledge and competencies needed to design and implement such responsive services and engagement strategies? What new partnerships will libraries invest in to create the capacities and reach needed to engage boomers? Finally, how will libraries address the preponderance of boomers in their own workforces and create flexible work options to retain experienced professional talent as teachers, mentors, and consultants to newly minted librarians?

Public library stewards, leaders, and professionals would be wise to heed the words of noted management guru Peter Drucker:

> Every few hundred years in western history there occurs a sharp transformation; within a few short decades, society rearranges itself—its worldview, its basic values, its social and political structure, its arts, its key institutions. Fifty years later, there is a new world. (1992)

REFERENCES

AARP. 2005. *The business case for workers age 50+: Planning for tomorrow's talent needs in today's competitive environment.* Report prepared for AARP by Towers Perrin. http://assets.aarp.org/rgcenter/econ/workers_fifty_plus_1.pdf.

AARP/Roper ASW. 2001. National telephone survey. www.aarp.org/research/surveys/stats/surveys/public/articles/aresearch-import-299.html.

Anthony, M. 2001. *The new retirementality.* Chicago: Dearborn Trade.

Casner-Lotto, J. 2007. *Boomers are ready for nonprofits but are nonprofits ready for them.* Conference Board. Report No. E-0012-07-WG. www.conference-board.org/publications/describe.cfm?id=1319.

Drucker, P. 1992. *The age of discontinuity.* Piscataway, NJ: Transaction Publishers.

Dychtwald, K. 2002. Age Wave/AIG Sun America Re-Visioning Retirement Project. www.agewave.com/research/landmark_revisioningRetirement.php.

Dychtwald, M. 2003. *Cycles: How we will live, work, and buy.* New York: Free Press.

Erikson, E. 1959. *Identity and the life cycle.* New York: International Universities Press.

Freedman, M. 1999. *Prime Time: How baby boomers will revolutionize retirement and transform America.* New York: Public Affairs.

———. 2007. *Encore.* New York: Public Affairs.

Freud, S. 2005. *Civilization and its discontents.* Introduction by Louis Menand. New York: W. W. Norton.

Gibran, K. 1923. *The prophet.* New York: Knopf.

Greller, M., and D. Nee. 1989. *From baby boom to baby bust.* New York: Addison-Wesley.

Kadlec, D. 2007. The do-gooder option. *Time,* November 2. www.time.com/time/magazine/article/0,9171,1680156,00.html.

McKendree, B. 2001. The container effect. *The Clarion Call* (Fall). www.theclarion group.com.

Moen, P. 1998. Recasting careers: Changing reference groups, risks, and realities. *Generations* (Spring): 40–45.

National Council on Aging. 2008. Respect*Ability* breaks new ground turning the age boom into the resource boom. www.ncoa.org/news-ncoa-publications/publications/final-respectability-ib1.pdf.

Retirement Reality Check. 2002. Allstate Financial/Harris Interactive. www.allstate.com.

Ristau, S., and Leadership Greater Hartford. 2003. *The career transition service leadership feasibility study.* Unpublished report.

Ristau, S., contrib. 2008. *The idealist guide to nonprofit careers for sector switchers,* 7. www.idealist.org/en/career/guide/sectorswitcher/index.html.

Savishinsky, J. 2000. *Breaking the watch: The meanings of retirement in America.* Ithaca, NY: Cornell University Press.

Terkel, S. 2005. *This I believe: Community in action.* National Public Radio. www.npr.org/templates/story/story.php?storyId=4963443.

PART TWO

INSTITUTIONAL OPORTUNITIES

IN SEARCH OF ACTIVE WISDOM

Libraries and Consciousness-Raising for Adulthood II

6

Mary Catherine Bateson

ACTIVE WISDOM

Active wisdom is the product of modern improvements in health that not only extend longevity but extend the years of relatively energetic and pain-free productivity and participation, creating a new life stage, Adulthood II, inserted before old age.

Wisdom comes from a lifetime of learning and reflecting on experience, but in the past wisdom was often associated with the waning strength and immobility of old age. Today's seniors often enjoy decades of energetic health that allow them to play active roles in society.

The convergence of *wisdom* and *activism* for large numbers of men and women in Adulthood II is a new phenomenon in human history. *Consciousness* of this phenomenon may be as revolutionary as the shifts in consciousness behind the liberation movements of the twentieth century.

With active wisdom we are talking not just about a systems change in the management of organizations or the development of social policies. We are talking about a systems change in the life of our species—a change in the meaning of what it is to be human. And it may be that none of us has grasped what that change means.

As we recognize and work with *active wisdom,* older Americans will discover not only the joys of social engagement but their ability to make unique contributions to a just and humane future.

A NEW LIFE STAGE: ADULTHOOD II

Most Americans are aware that the baby boom generation is now beginning to reach retirement age, creating a variety of new demands. Less widely understood is that this is happening at a time when *retirement* has changed its meaning, and both the population and the individual life cycle have taken on a new structure. Yes, there will be more 65-year-olds and, over time, more 70-, 80-, and 90-year-olds. But for over a decade it has been clear that today's 70-year-olds are very different from 70-year-olds of the past. The implications of these differences have not yet taken root in our thinking.

Government retirement pensions were invented in Germany at the beginning of the twentieth century, at a time when 65- and 70-year-olds were few and far between (life expectancy at birth was about 45), were mostly very limited in their ability to work, and would not be around for long. In other words, retirement was invented for people whose conditions were in many ways worse than those of 95-year-olds today. Today's 65-year-olds are starting new careers or continuing old ones, traveling around the world, and eloping with new loves. They have the potential for altering public life in America.

There has been extensive discussion of how much the retirement of the boomers will cost and how far pensions and medical insurance will be stretched, looking at extended longevity as a liability. In effect, there has been a glaring failure of imagination, a failure to see that, because today's older adults have health and energy and resources, they represent a new resource for society and that retirement offers new opportunities and choices in composing their lives. This societal failure of imagination has affected individuals coming up on retirement as well, both in overemphasizing future needs and deficits and in failing to appreciate possibilities and potentials. It also affects the way they look at others of the same age and makes them hesitant to join other older adults to influence society's future in ways that are often not open to younger adults.

We all use our parents and grandparents, to some degree, as models, even though their experiences have come to seem less relevant. Will I be the same kind of parent as my mom or dad? Most new parents today plan to do many things differently than their own parents. Today's 60-somethings remember their own grandparents as elderly, but they are just beginning to understand that they will not become elderly in the same way and at the same pace and, above all, that they must discover or invent brand-new ways of living for the years that remain, often as many as thirty or forty—far too many to spend on golf, television, and bridge.

Forty years ago, young women looking at their lives, with the newly developed possibility of planning their childbearing, discovered the need to break out of inherited assumptions about who they were, what they could do, and what they wanted in their lives. They had been trained to imagine their futures in terms of a set of culturally constructed stereotypes and to desire what society was ready to give them. In learning to want something more and different, reading was critical, reflection was critical, but above all the process required conversation. In fact, in each of the American liberation movements of the twentieth century—the civil rights movement, gay liberation, the women's movement, the disabilities awareness movement—an entire group of people had to learn to look at themselves differently. They had to find opportunities to shape new answers to the questions "Who am I?" "What is the meaning of my life?" "What am I worth?"

Today, men and women approaching retirement (and the cohorts that will follow them) with newly granted health and longevity face the same challenge: to achieve a new kind of consciousness and to free their imaginations for the future. The same kind of process of conversation is needed now.

We have to begin to think of a new developmental stage inserted into the life cycle, not the extension of old age. Ten years ago I called it second adulthood, but that phrase too easily evokes the second-rate or secondhand. We need, now, to think of a first adult stage we can call Adulthood I—a very busy time, in which productivity and generativity include for most of us both our primary child-rearing years and the building of careers—and a stage called Adulthood II, which is new in human history.

Adulthood II does not fit an exact chronological rule but may begin as early as 40 and extend past 80, for many years of participation and contribution. Many in this age group are grandparents, but not in quite the same way as their own grandparents. They adore their grandchildren, but they are not sitting still. They will not behave like the stereotype of grandparents—long memories and short walks—until they are great-grandparents. From a society of children, parents, and grandparents, we are shifting into a four-generation society of children, parents (Adulthood I), grandparents (Adulthood II), and great-grandparents. Figure 6.1 shows (1) a traditional three-generation structure in which there are a few living great-grandparents, but both grandparents and great-grandparents play the role of elders; and (2) a four-generation society in which increasing good health and numbers have led to a differentiation in roles for grandparents and great-grandparents. Figures 6.2 and 6.3 shows an alternative way of looking at these same patterns. The figures offer not only a display of different stages but also a way of seeing a change in the simultaneities: for instance, in a three-generation society adults are caring for their aging parents and their young children at the same time, while in a four-generation society those same

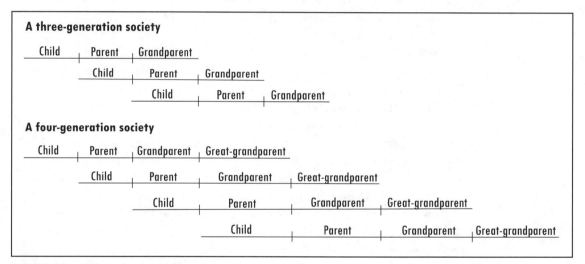

FIGURE 6.1   Child, parent, grandparent chart

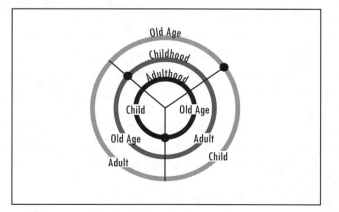

FIGURE 6.2   A three-generation society

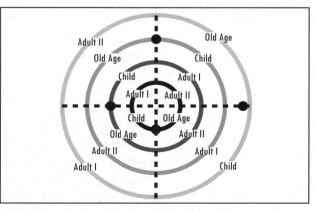

FIGURE 6.3   A four-generation society

parents are still active, often working and caring for their own parents, and both less available and less dependent than they were in the past.

What is the significance of increasing numbers of grandparents and great-grandparents? Research comparing different human groups living in comparable environments shows that the chances of survival of newborns are increased if they have living grandparents. It doesn't just take a village, it takes a three-generation village to raise human beings. We are now becoming a four-generation village. This shift has implications for our perceptions of Adulthood II and for the overall societal possibilities of a multigenerational population.

There are other potential implications of a society with an increasing proportion of older adults with a lifetime of experiences and perspectives. Just as the extension of childhood made possible a whole new order of learning and adaptability in human beings, so does the extension of lives beyond biological procreation have the potential for changing the way we make decisions as a society, the way we think about the present, and the way we think about the past. If, for instance, our responsibility as human beings is to think beyond our own lifetimes, then we should be able to benefit from the longer-term perspectives of older adults who have had to learn and relearn, adapt and develop, and look backward and forward over their various life stages.

For example, the only way we will be able, responsibly and humanely, to address the environmental disruptions of climate change, which can still be mitigated but not prevented, is by thinking of a time span longer than any of our own lifetimes. Caring for future generations is linked to this longer-term imperative: caring about one's grandchildren, one's great-grandchildren, one's nieces and nephews, the neighbor's children, the unknown children to come—this is the way to think about the future, and it is a way in which older people can and will think and engage.

When we speak about the active wisdom that can be realized and active in Adulthood II, we are talking about a shift in who we are as a species, in what it means to be human. We are talking about changing our own thinking in very deep ways that underscore the importance of reflection, discussion, and consciousness-raising.

When do you move from Adulthood I to Adulthood II? When you realize that you have done a lot of what you hoped to do in life but that it is not too late to do something more or different. The doorway to this new stage of life is not filing for Social Security but thinking differently and continuing to learn. Adulthood II adds the wisdom associated with long lives and rich experience to the energy and commitment of youth in the context of a new freedom from day-to-day responsibility.

The best name I have been able to find for this approach is *Active Wisdom.* Wisdom is the most positive and valued trait of people who live long lives. It is also the most acceptable word for talking about old age. The challenge is to stimulate imaginations to combine that wisdom with activity and social engagement to make it effective in one's life and in the world.

The vital question about seniors does not concern the state of their health or their income or their housing arrangements, although these are all very important. The critical question is this: Have we created a society that truly supports lifelong learning and that benefits from the perspective, the tolerance for ambiguity, the willingness to rethink and reimagine that are functions of reflection and conversation in Adulthood II?

LIBRARIES AS PARTNERS IN THE SEARCH FOR ACTIVE WISDOM

It is the mission of libraries to stretch imaginations beyond a particular time and place, and America needs help in reimagining the future shape of lives.

America's libraries can become the forum for this process of reimagining, which, like the consciousness-raising of the sixties, must rest on learning, reflection, and conversation. This process belongs in places where people feel safe and know that they can find respect for diversity of opinion, background, and interest. It belongs also in places that span generations, as libraries do, because the new thought process will not happen in a context where individuals are slotted by age expectations and should not be limited to those who have already retired. It needs to happen locally within communities so conversation can be sustained and extended beyond particular programs. And it needs to happen in a context where recreation can mean more than entertainment.

Active Wisdom Conversations have been piloted in a few locations; the concept is poised for further development and experimentation across the country. Such a program can be a touchstone for individuals as they discover Adulthood II and can provide a framework for groups as they explore their next life phases. It could lead to proposals for social action and civic engagement originating in the group.

Active Wisdom Conversations help raise participants' consciousness about the value and meaning of their own life experiences (wisdom) and how these can be developed and applied in a new (active) phase of adulthood. Most of us care about the world beyond our own lifetimes, so older adults need to feel that they have the right to hold and voice opinions about issues going beyond their own welfare and to claim the wisdom to contribute to decisions.

Any change in consciousness requires its own process, leading to action with increasing clarity. Active Wisdom Conversations are therefore the beginning of a process that can lead to individual action or even social action and community engagement.

Public libraries differ greatly from community to community, so there is a need for a variety of pilot programs in different kinds of settings and for experimentation with different formats. Through the Lifelong Access Libraries initiative of Libraries for the Future, several Lifelong Access Fellows have started Active Wisdom Conversations in communities across the country. Their experiences provide initial guidance for other library experiments.

The process for starting Active Wisdom Conversations should be straightforward and simple. It should (a) orient participants to the setting and one another, (b) encourage participants to start reimagining themselves and the process of aging, and (c) provide just enough structure to foster trust and collegiality.

A reading or a film can be useful in providing participants with a common experience and the basis for an open discussion. An announced topic can stimulate curiosity and thinking in advance. For some people, taking part in conversations that are self-reflective and imaginative, with strangers or neighbors, may come easily. For most of us, however, it is easier to approach life issues indirectly through a common experience or idea. Librarians and community or academic advisors can identify texts, topics, and films that are useful in stimulating reflection and life analysis, especially if facilitators draw the threads together at the end and suggest a direction for reflection prior to the next meeting.

Whatever approach your library selects—topics, films, readings—and whatever questions your conversation leader poses, they are inevitably going to touch on fairly personal matters, and it may take time for trust to develop. As people begin to speak about their own lives, it must be understood that what they say is private to the group. Each person's contribution is respected. Alternatives and visions of the possibilities are useful, but criticisms and rigid prescriptions are not. People do not become more similar as they grow older, as stereotypes suggest—they become more individual.

Whether conversations are organized around a series of questions, topics, or literary works, the goal is to prompt open-ended reflection, emphasizing the positive rather than limitations. Although it is important and inevitable that problems will be discussed, part of the facilitator's task is to encourage the search for possibilities, especially through synergies. For example, taking a part-time job is not only a way to supplement income; it is also a way to find new friends and discover new talents. It is often useful to encourage analogies with earlier experiences and successful adaptations, so talking about the past not only evokes nostalgia but engages resources. Anyone who has lived half a century or more in this country is a veteran of the processes of change and new learning, but not everyone ends up in the same place.

The setting and structure for Active Wisdom Conversations can influence participants' comfort level and willingness to contribute. Ideally, you should provide a relatively private space for the group discussion, and the group itself should not be too large. The meeting place should allow ten to twenty people to gather and converse without interruption. Schedule the conversations for one and a half to two hours. It is helpful to start each session after the first with a go-around of thoughts since the last meeting and to end with a go-around for summary (what will you take with you?) and afterthoughts (what needs further discussion?).

If possible, schedule Active Wisdom Conversations at a time when people who have not retired from regular jobs can come and spend up to two hours, along with others whose schedules are more flexible. There should be a clear beginning and end to each session. The program should run for a limited time, such as once a week for two months. Encourage participants to continue after that time in private homes or with a peer leader at the library.

With respect to who leads Active Wisdom Conservations, there are many choices and room for experimentation. A facilitator or host is needed to start things off and establish a self-sustaining pattern, but the principal task of the facilitator is to engage the whole group. The best leader is someone who hopes to learn from the group, not someone who has all the answers. The goal is to create a process that encourages trust and participation. The most obvious candidates are (a) a member of the library staff, regardless of age; (b) a library volunteer, especially a member of an advisory council who has an interest in new programming for older adults; (c) someone with a professional understanding of aging issues (here I would recommend a student rather than a traditional gerontologist); or (d) an older adult library patron who is comfortable working with groups and is interested in Active Wisdom. Most librarians will know at least one regular patron who has been actively reading about this subject and would respond to an invitation—and if such a person is not found at the start, one or several will emerge as the program continues. Supply a start-up reading list for whoever undertakes this task.

It is helpful to move forward with the program in stages. The first event might be informational, with a film or brief discussion to introduce the series, and open to the public. A committee of three or four might plan an open session to which a slightly larger audience would be attracted. People often need the chance to get a taste before making any kind of commitment. At the first session, offer the chance to sign up for subsequent sessions. Some groups may wish to remain open to new members while others may prefer greater continuity.

When a group has met for the full series of six, eight, or ten sessions, ask members how they would like to continue. Some groups may decide to continue independently, with participants taking turns or selecting a peer to become the convener for the next iteration. Such groups may take on action projects of one sort or another, but even if the emphasis changes it is wise to retain the opportunity for reflection and discussion.

Whatever the particular structure, group leader, or means of initiating the Active Wisdom Conversations, it will be important to refocus every session around the fundamental question of Adulthood II and participants' capacities to reshape their own lives, to improve the lives of others, and to stimulate new solutions for societal problems affecting future generations. At the same time, the leader should not have a rigid agenda and should be sensitive to emerging themes, allowing the group to veer to other topics if the interest seems to be shared. There are no right or wrong answers here.

LOOKING AHEAD

Hosting one or two series of Active Wisdom Conversations will not fulfill the potential of libraries as sites for consciousness-raising about Adulthood II. Ideally, the Active Wisdom Conversations will set in motion a process of further reflection and inquiry.

To assist in this process, the library has numerous resources at hand. It will be helpful to set out relevant books and periodicals, including fiction, memoirs, and poetry, and to develop a traditional readers' advisory service specifically for participants. A web page with resources for further inquiry and online exchange on the conversation topic will be a stimulus to reflection that goes beyond those who are present for discussions, as would be a special Active Wisdom section, to which program participants and other readers can return again and again. In addition, depending on space and numbers, peer-led, small-group conversations or breakout groups can evolve into performances and readings, community project planning, and all sorts of reflective or action-oriented activities to advance consciousness-raising. Given the disproportionately problem-oriented discussion of aging, it is important to emphasize the positive aspects of aging and the contributions of Active Wisdom not only in the conversations but in related library activities.

In the twenty-first century, becoming wise doesn't mean being confined to a rocking chair. It doesn't mean barely being able to move across the room. In the twenty-first century, becoming wise means being active, contributing to society, and going beyond independence to interdependence. Libraries are places where people can discuss and totally change their understanding of who they are and what their potentials are. Active Wisdom Conversations are a good place to begin. Active wisdom is not about the past. It is a critical resource for the future.

INFORMATION-QUESTING MOMENTS

Retirement-Age Americans at the Library Door

Ronald J. Manheimer and Miwako Kidahashi

Life changes often spark the need for information. From books about baby names to periodicals on investing during a bear market, key personal and societal transitions trigger questions that motivate decision makers to seek out the facts and puzzle over their meaning. Sometimes they go to friends and relatives or purported experts, sometimes to the Internet, and sometimes they walk into their neighborhood public library. Contemplating choices concerning how, when, or whether to retire will similarly send people scurrying for relevant resources. The public library should be one of these resources.

Until the middle of the twentieth century, retirement was not an especially troubling event that would qualify as an information-questing moment. True, the average age of retirement in the United States had been gradually declining for decades. But the lifestyle choices following child rearing and occupational pursuits were limited. Photo albums depicted grandparents hugging grandchildren on arrival at their adult children's homes, driving cross-country in their aluminum-clad Airstream trailers, or setting out on the golf links with friends. Retiring meant showing up for your workplace bon voyage party, receiving an award for dedicated service, and receiving that first Social Security check. For most women who were not working outside the home, retirement meant preparing that infamous "honey-do" list for a seemingly aimless spouse.

Around 1960, the slow-moving change accelerated, and a new image of the post-retirement, leisure lifestyle pervaded the culture. Now thousands of people began looking for ways to fill a longer, healthier, and more financially secure period that was to be dubbed the "third age" (Laslett 1989). Going back to work appealed to many who either needed extra money or found an unstructured life without work demands tedious or boring. Others turned avocations into semi- or full vocations. Volunteering offered the moral equivalent of paid work and a way to meet new friends. The 1970s saw a sharp increase in older persons' participation in educational programs—mainly of the noncredit or informal type (Manheimer 2008).

Retirement has become a lengthy process, rather than an event. It's now a whole chunk of the life course. Some people do it repeatedly, and some, not at all. The term, which has no accurate or nontrivial substitute, has taken on multiple meanings associated with diverse pathways ranging from complete withdrawal from the workplace and a life dedicated to leisure to mixing paid work with travel, family outings, and recreation. For those who belong to the "sandwich generation," it may mean taking on unexpected responsibilities for both adult children and grandchildren. Thousands of books and hundreds of magazines and websites testify to the market for advice about retirement-related issues such as finances, housing, relocation, health, travel, and even how to be a more effective grandparent.

There is no cultural consensus about what one is supposed to do in the retirement period. AARP surveys indicate that the cessation of work will increasingly be delayed (AARP 2004). Using reflection to draw on one's knowledge and experience and making a "strategic selection" seem to be the order of the day (Moen and Spencer 2006). Couples have to negotiate their preferences, and singles often seek out friends and professional advisors for help. So-called professional life coaching for midlife adults has become a burgeoning field of employment. Self-organizing groups such as the Transition Network (Transition Network and Rentsch 2008) have cropped up to offer moral support, insight, information, and guidance on how to go through a transition process that triggers important questions about identity, authority, purpose, relationships, money, physical changes, and spiritual well-being.

CONCEPTUAL FRAMEWORKS FOR RETIREMENT

How then should library professionals understand the opportunities for meeting the needs of the millions of people for whom the third age poses more challenges than the drama of adolescence or the bewildering possibilities of post-college adult life? Numerous frameworks abound. For example, following the work of generations researchers William Strauss and Neil Howe (1991), a whole new cadre of consultants began touring the country to announce that generational characteristics were the key determinants of values and, therefore, buying preferences of individuals labeled as members of the civic, silent, boomer, X, and Y generations. Others countered that you could learn more about people by knowing their functional abilities. Were they the young-old, old, or oldest of the old? Gender and sexual orientation would also have to be taken into account. And what about psychographic attributes (attitudes linked to personality and social class) that may or may not be attributed to generational effects? As professional librarians well know, every classification system has its assets and deficiencies for making the world more intelligible.

Each conceptual framework represents an attempt to put some order and predictability into the way we look at the historically unprecedented demographic shift that is making the United States and many other postindustrial countries "aging societies." The key principle implied by all these attempts to formulate a paradigm of the "new aging" is diversity. Each generalization or framework is useful . . . to a point. Up in the air is the question of whether the third age marks a definitive life stage with unique characteristics (Dychtwald 1999; Freedman 1999, 2007; Handy 1989; Sadler 2006) or is more accurately a blurred extension of midlife in which the continuity of an "ageless self" is more apparent than is a dramatic transformation of values and lifestyle (Atchley 1992; Kaufman 1986).

THE LIFE COURSE MODEL APPROACH

Given the preceding caveats, we propose a life course model approach that may help library professionals to seize the information-questing moment. For here is an opportunity to both serve regular patrons and attract new ones while strengthening connections to community residents poised in a unique time of both perplexity and excitement.

Our model focuses on the choice of whether to seek work for pay as a key variable (work/nonwork orientation) along with whether one's choice indicates a new or existing/traditional value orientation. Figure 7.1 identifies five life course models.

These life models are exactly that—models that are highly simplified and separate types that, in reality, may overlap. They highlight the diverse ways people are engaging in some form of "productive aging" (Butler and Gleason 1985). The category labeled Traditional Golden Years points to a lifestyle in which leisure is highly valued. We may think of advertisements for retirement communities that emphasize relaxing activities such as golf, swimming, tennis, fishing, bridge, and so on. The category Neo-Golden Years points to an added emphasis on searching for meaning and pursuing self-development, whether through independent study, informal learning groups, or enrollment in credit-bearing college courses. The Portfolio Life category aims at balance—between some form of work for pay and time for family, travel, recreation, and other valued activities. The Second Career orientation includes several possibilities—turning a former hobby into an income-generating occupation, joining a business launched by adult children, or pursuing an "encore career" (Freedman 2007) in which one segues to a type of work that offers significant benefit to society, such as teaching high school or working for a nonprofit social action group. Finally,

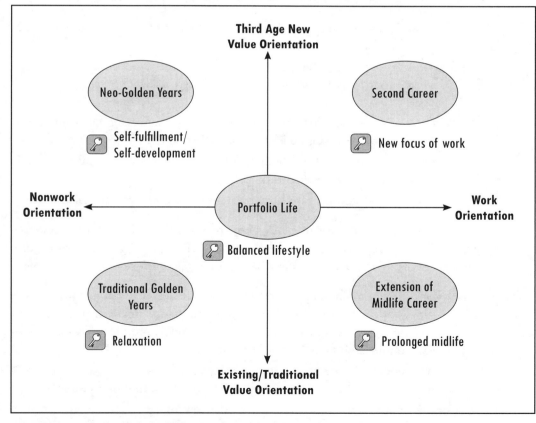

FIGURE 7.1   Typology of ideal life course models in later life

the Extension of Midlife Career category describes a person who wants to extend his or her current work activity for as long as possible, whether motivated by money, status and the preservation of identity, the creative satisfaction of the work at hand, or a combination of all three.

The New Value orientation gauges whether a person's choice implies a major change in prized activity. So if you had been working eight-to-ten-hour days as a small-business owner and then retired to lead a relaxing, unstressed life filled with recreation and travel, the choice would imply a major change in activity patterns and life goal orientation. If, however, you sought the Portfolio Life, you would be seeking a more moderate change that preserves some of the characteristics of an existing Midlife Career orientation while opting for elements of the less stressful work-centered life, such as time for travel and family activities.

OPPORTUNITIES FOR LIBRARIES AND LIBRARIANS

Each lifestyle type involves a certain degree of intentional and informed choice. As people contemplate whether, when, and how they are going to alter the amount and intensity of time spent on work for pay as they explore a new mixture of leisure, recreation, travel, family time, volunteering, and lifelong learning, they will experience acute information needs. This is a window of opportunity for public libraries. Consider the possible learning and, therefore, information needs of the five types.

> *Traditional Goldens*—resources for getting more out of leisure activities such as travel, recreation, hobbies, sports
>
> *Neo-Goldens*—resources for pursuing cultural and educational enrichment, socialization, some new skills, self-qualifying certificate such as master gardener
>
> *Portfolios*—information for updating career skills, identifying part-time career opportunities, learning to lead a more balanced life
>
> *Second Careers*—information about how to start new businesses, pursue socially beneficial "encore careers," turn an avocation into a vocation
>
> *Work Extenders*—resources for learning skills to keep up professional abilities

Library leaders will want to explore how to make their library's resources especially visible to individuals traversing the information-questing moment of retirement decision making. Here are a few ideas for linking resources with individuals.

> Develop programs in support of retirement transition planning, including a series with invited experts (e.g., career counselors, financial planners, psychologists) or a self-facilitated discussion/support group with an appropriately trained and knowledgeable facilitator
>
> Prepare annotated guides to print and electronic resources concerning retirement, lifelong learning, grandparenting, health promotion in midlife
>
> Organize a film series on changing attitudes toward aging and retirement, such as the Elderquest series (www.lets.umb.edu/elderquest/)

Offer age-neutral programs likely to appeal to a 50+ audience who have the time to explore new learning opportunities and to meet people with similar interests

Provide a tool kit for the new retirement: what everyone needs to know about entitlement programs (e.g., Medicare, Social Security), housing options, ways to reenter the workforce, fitness programs, free or inexpensive recreational activities

To plan and implement these types of activities, library leaders should include other organizations in partnership and collaboration. Partnering organizations could include councils on aging, senior centers, hospital wellness programs, fitness centers, museums, lifelong learning programs at colleges and universities, travel agencies, financial services companies, and so on. Certainly, it would be ideal to recruit knowledgeable and engaged retirees themselves who might be willing to play volunteer leadership roles and who would have relevant expertise, such as marketing, communications, education, event planning, and, if needed, grant writing.

REFERENCES

AARP. 2004. *Baby boomers envision retirement II: Survey of baby boomers' expectations for retirement.* www.aarp.org/research/surveys/stats/demo/boomers/articles/aresearch-import-865.html

Atchley, R. 1992. Critical perspectives on retirement. In *Voices and visions of aging: Toward a critical gerontology,* ed. T. Cole, A. Achenbaum, P. Jakobi, and R. Kastenbaum. New York: Springer.

Butler, R., and H. Gleason. 1985. *Productive aging: Enhancing vitality in later life.* New York: Springer.

Dychtwald, K. 1999. *Age power.* New York: Jeremy P. Tarcher/Putnam.

Freedman, M. 1999. *Prime time: How baby boomers will revolutionize retirement and transform America.* New York: Public Affairs.

———. 2007. *Encore.* New York: Public Affairs.

Handy, C. 1989. *The age of unreason.* Boston: Harvard Business School Press.

Kaufman, S. 1986. *The ageless self: Sources of meaning in late life.* New York: Meridian.

Laslett, P. 1989. *A fresh map of life.* Cambridge, MA: Harvard University Press.

Manheimer, R. 2008. Gearing up for the big show: Lifelong learning programs are coming of age. In *Boomer bust? Economic and political issues of the graying society,* ed. R. Hudson. Westport, CT: Praeger Perspectives.

Moen, P., and D. Spencer. 2006. Converging divergences in age, gender, health, and well-being: Strategic selection in the third age. In *Handbook of aging and the social sciences,* ed. R. Binstock and L. George. 6th ed. Amsterdam: Elsevier.

Sadler, W. 2006. Changing life options: Uncovering the riches of the third age. *LLI Review* (Fall).

Strauss, W., and N. Howe. 1991. *Generations: The history of America's future, 1584 to 2069.* New York: Harper.

Transition Network and G. Rentsch. 2008. *Smart women don't retire—they break free.* Boston: Springboard Press.

RECONSIDERING AGE
The Emerging Role of Cultural Institutions

8

Diantha Dow Schull and Selma Thomas

BACKGROUND

The extension of the human life span is one of the greatest demographic and social transformations in American history. As late as 1790, only 20 percent of Americans lived to age 70. Today, with improved nutrition and medical care, more than 80 percent can expect to do so. At the dawn of the twentieth century, the average life span of an American was 49 years. Today, it has extended to 75 years, and it appears likely to keep extending. This is the "longevity revolution," defined by Dr. Robert N. Butler, preeminent social gerontologist, in *The Longevity Revolution: The Benefits and Challenges of Living a Long Life.* Longevity is fast becoming a focus of attention not only for gerontologists but also for economists, community planners, marketers, and the media (Butler 2008).

Increased longevity is only one part of the bio-demographic changes affecting social and economic life. What some call the "elder boom" has just begun. Older people comprise approximately 13 percent of our population today, but by the middle of this century, more than 20 percent of the American population will be over 65, and 5 percent will be over 85. In some regions and states, the proportions will be even greater.

Over the next decades, these trends will profoundly impact every aspect of American life, from housing and work to ethics and civic life. Yet, the national discourse on aging and longevity focuses primarily on the biological and economic dimensions. Planning and policy making are centered on such issues as the fiscal health of Social Security and Medicare and the need for providing more suitable retirement living and long-term custodial care. Beyond these issues, however, lie deeper questions that challenge the cultural expectations of all Americans, young and old.

The lack of humanistic perspectives in the national discourse on aging has societal implications. Longevity will require preparation for extended life spans. Without exposure to past experiences of aging, representations of aging, and examples of older adults in varied roles and cultural settings, it will be harder for people to develop models for living and participating throughout older adulthood. Without opportunities to reflect on aging as a potentially positive aspect of the human life cycle, it will be harder for people to shed stereotypes of older adults and create new approaches to aging. Without an awareness of past aging policies, it will be harder to imagine and develop policies for an aging society.

A number of leading scholars have expressed concern about the lack of multidisciplinary perspectives in the national discourse on aging. Dr. Robert Butler states, "Both the philosophy of childhood and the philosophy of old age have been neglected. We need guides that help us live out our lives, enjoy longevity, and contribute responsibly to others in the later years" (Butler 2008, 400). Anthropologist Mary Catherine Bateson, in a recent interview, speaks of "obsolete definitions of aging that we have to move away from. . . . Each one of us needs to rethink the things we take for granted about different ages and aging, and the first step is to become conscious of what it is we already think and then examine that against reality" (Bateson 2008).

THE ROLE OF CULTURAL INSTITUTIONS

Cultural institutions are key resources for broadening our understanding of aging. Their collections contain works of art, writings, recordings, artifacts, and other forms of human expression that document varied experiences and interpretations of aging. Their audiences and their communities are further sources of images, memories, and accounts of aging. Cultural institutions can draw on humanists and artists who bring varied disciplinary and cultural perspectives, and through their programming they can illuminate concepts of aging across time and place.

Library and museum programs take many forms. Most libraries offer literature programs, film festivals, exhibits, lectures, book discussions, and community forums, while museums may offer gallery talks, art classes, video presentations, performances, and even artists-in-residence. Both libraries and museums conduct programs off-site, with outreach to individuals and groups in a wide variety of community and educational settings. Both are active contributors to and participants in digital networks of information and social networking. All these program formats and modes of communication offer opportunities to stimulate reflection and dialogue on aging.

By presenting and interpreting representations of age and aging, and by stimulating conversations about their meaning and relevance, cultural institutions can help to counter traditional stereotypes and promote awareness of the historical and cultural circumstances that determine our attitudes about aging.

PAVING THE WAY

Despite the potential to expand understanding of aging, few libraries or museums have focused on aging as a subject for interpretation. Curators, librarians, and cultural institution leaders have not examined their collections through the lens of "age," nor have they gathered and interpreted the historical and cultural memories of their constituents and communities with respect to long-held beliefs about age and aging.

One exhibition project, Images of Old Age in America: 1790 to the Present, stands out as an exception. Images of Old Age was an exhibition and publication organized under the auspices of the Institute of Gerontology at the University of Michigan in 1978. Cocurated by Dr. Andrew Achenbaum, a historian then teaching at Canisius College, and Peggy Ann Kusnerz, audiovisual materials coordinator for the University of Michigan, Images of Old Age presented prints and photographs first exhibited in Ann Arbor during a Festival of Aging and the Art of Living (Achenbaum and Kusnerz 1978). That exhibition became the basis for an exhibition catalog and a traveling exhibition circulated nationwide to museums and libraries by the Smithsonian Institution Traveling Exhibition Service (SITES).

Images of Old Age brought together photographs and graphic images documenting "continuities and changes over time in representations of older Americans" drawn from collections of libraries, museums, and historical agencies across the country. Historian-curator Achenbaum's premise was that changing American perceptions about aging would be reflected in visual materials of historical significance. According to both curators, this thesis proved correct. Exhibition research showed that "the changing perceptions about aging reflected in written accounts and literature . . . were also evident in collateral visual artifacts" (Achenbaum and Kusnerz 1978, viii).

Images of Old Age is both an art and a history exhibit, with the images accompanied by quotes reflecting the attitudes of the time. Some of the images are landmarks of photography or graphic art. Most are more common images such as Currier and Ives prints, daguerreotypes, magazine illustrations, or photographs commissioned by the federal government as part of the WPA project.

Dr. Achenbaum, in his introduction to Images of Old Age, discusses some of the lessons learned through his attempts to "illustrate the extent to which value systems have determined perceptions of the elderly over time." One of the fundamental lessons underscores the need for exposure to images and accounts that counter contemporary prejudices.

> A basic discontinuity between the images and realities of growing old, in fact, regrettably characterizes our own time. Most Americans subscribe to negative ideas of older people, which once seemed to make sense, but which no longer have any basis in fact. (Achenbaum and Kusnerz 1978, viii)

Twenty years later, in 1998, SITES circulated another exhibition focusing on older adults, entitled Going Strong: Older Americans on the Job. Going Strong consisted of images by photographer Harvey Wang, who spent a decade capturing the faces, hands, and stories of men and women at varied worksites. He depicted older workers who remained dedicated to their occupations long past "retirement" age.

A different kind of humanities project, the Silver Editions Project, took place in the early 1990s under the auspices of the National Council on Aging with support from the National Endowment for the Humanities (Liroff and Van Fleet 1992). Local scholars in geographically dispersed library systems around the country led discussion groups made up of twenty to twenty-five older adults, offering opportunities to discuss literacy and historical and philosophical themes such as "The Remembered Past: 1914–1945" and "The Search for Meaning: Insights through Literature, History, and Art."

These three projects stand out as late-twentieth-century efforts by cultural institutions to promote public attention to the humanistic dimensions of aging. It is only now, a decade into the twenty-first century, that we see such projects expanding and new attention being paid to aging on the part of our libraries, museums, and historical agencies.

CURRENT TRENDS

With the advent of the twenty-first century and the beginning of the longevity revolution, cultural institution leaders have begun to realize that they have powerful roles to play—as humanists, historians, art historians, educators, archivists, curators, and librarians—in stimulating creative responses to an aging society. In recent years a handful of institutions—primarily museums—have created exhibitions that suggest the possibilities for cultural institutions to both provoke and participate in emerging discussions on age and aging.

The Art of Aging was an international exhibition of eighty-two works by contemporary artists from North America, Israel, and England held at Hebrew Union College–Jewish Institute of Religion Museum in New York City in 2003–2004 (http://huc.edu/newspubs/pressroom/2003/aging.shtml). Curated by Laura Kruger, the exhibition explored the ways in which "aging is a process that begins with birth . . . a lifelong journey affecting the dynamics of human relationships, creativity, memory, continuity, and growth." The exhibition was accompanied by numerous public programs, including conversations with some of the artists represented in the exhibit, talks by writers, lectures by specialists in "wisdom literature" and creativity, a seminar on Cultural Representations of Aging, staged readings of a play, and a musical production titled "Give Me Time."

Exhibiting Signs of Age was shown at the Berkeley (California) Museum of Arts in the fall of 2003 and the Colby College Museum of Art (Waterville, Maine) in the winter and spring of 2004. The show explored representations of aging in twentieth-century art, featuring photographs and works on paper by eleven artists, ranging from Louise Nevelson, Robert Mapplethorpe, and George Segal to Chester Higgins Jr. and Chuck Close (http://bampfa.berkeley.edu/press/release/TXT0070).

Golden Blessings of Old Age and Out of the Mouths of Babes were linked exhibitions shown at the American Visionary Art Museum/Baltimore Museum of Art from October 2003 to September 2004. Golden Blessings of Old Age featured examples of late-onset creativity generated by visionary artists ages 60–80 and beyond, while Out of the Mouths of Babes consisted of depictions of childhood by Baltimore youth. The exhibition announcement stated, "Rigid notions of age and aging limit the mind and imprison the spirit. . . . Only by teasing apart the stereotypes can we truly see the individual members of the invisible old and the unheard young" (www.avam.org/exhibitions/blessings.html).

Elder Grace: The Nobility of Aging and Passing the Legacy: Reflections of Our Elders formed another pair of linked exhibitions, presented by the New York State Museum in Albany from October 2004 through April 2005 (www.nysm.nysed.gov/press/2004/elder.cfm). Elder Grace, originally organized by the New-York Historical Society, consisted of fifty photographs taken by Chester Higgins Jr. to honor African American men and women who "are experiencing aging with energy, wit and grace." Higgins, a *New York Times* photographer, aimed to "encourage us as a society to stop denigrating ourselves, to embrace the natural signs of aging," and to "glory in the strength of mind and character gained from years of living." Passing the Legacy consisted of photo portraits of eleven Albany-area residents who had made significant contributions to the Capital District as older adults.

Aside from exhibitions, other kinds of program formats are part of the emerging trend toward cultural programming on aging, including book discussions, film programs, creative performances, and video productions. Although there is not yet a national "Let's Talk about It" book discussion series on aging, a number of local libraries and state humanities councils have developed discussion themes that directly or indirectly focus on aging. Reading America, a national intercultural and intergenerational program developed by Libraries for the Future with funding from the MetLife Foundation, resulted in local programming in libraries, museums, and historical societies in North Dakota, Phoenix, and Dallas. The Reading America projects featured older adults as assets with memories to share through tours, oral histories, and community conversations with young people.

The California Humanities Council's California Story Program supported EngAGE Across Generations: The Art of Active Aging, in which older adults and at-risk youth in Burbank (California) cocreated videos about each other's life experiences (http://calhum.org/programs/story_engage.htm). The Passage of Time, the Meaning of Change: Perspectives by Five Writers from Maine is a book discussion series supported by the Maine Humanities Council that explores change over time from individual and community perspectives (http://mainehumanities.org/programs/talk-passage-of-time.html), and the National Endowment for the Humanities awarded a grant to the University of Massachusetts' Learning in Retirement Program to develop Elderquest, a curriculum on aging in film (www.lets.umb.edu/elderquest/).

The state of Nebraska is embarking on one of the most substantial book discussions to date through a three-part series, Growing Older in Nebraska (www.nebraska humanities.org/programs/agingpopulation.html). These discussions will take place in libraries and other community agencies as part of a larger initiative that explores the impact of demographic changes in the state. Developed by the Nebraska Humanities Council, this program challenges citizens to read critically, bearing in mind such questions as "What will be the role of our aging citizens? Will Nebraska be a state of elders—those having authority by virtue of age and experience, according to the Merriam-Webster Dictionary—or of the simply elderly?"

All these public program examples reflect an emerging trend and point to the potential for cultural institutions to help shape new attitudes about age and aging in America.

AGE IN AMERICA: A WORK IN PROGRESS

In 2005, recognizing the opportunities for libraries and museums to contribute to discussions on aging, we initiated a national project, Age in America: Expanding Public Understanding of Aging through Museum-Library Collaboration (www.age inamerica.org). Age in America is a two-year national demonstration program that engages museums and libraries in development and testing of public programs on age and aging in America. Three local projects involving museum-library collaboration are demonstrating approaches for programming that illuminate the changing roles and representations of older adults in the home, the workplace, and the community.

Age in America was developed initially under the aegis of Libraries for the Future and is being carried out by the Reimagining Age Project, a nonprofit dedicated to promoting public investigation of age and aging from historical, artistic, and policy perspectives. Projects are taking place in three diverse communities with growing populations of older adults: Hartford, Connecticut; Suffolk County, New York; and Norfolk, Virginia.

The primary goal of Age in America is to demonstrate the potential for museums and libraries, working together both locally and nationally, to strengthen public understanding of aging as a historical and cultural phenomenon. The project examines definitions, representations, and experiences of aging in diverse communities and different periods, and it provides a framework for understanding the historical and cultural dimensions of aging. It also positions libraries and museums as partners in an effort to illuminate a significant contemporary issue.

Funded by the Institute of Museum and Library Services, a federal agency, Age in America is based on an earlier planning phase funded by the National Endowment for the Humanities and the Petersmeyer Family Foundation.

During Age in America planning, organizers worked with an interdisciplinary panel of advisors who articulated the themes for the national program. They affirmed the concept that age is both a personal experience and a cultural phenomenon—and should be addressed as both. Further, they affirmed the need for a community-based discussion, one that might address both the stereotypes and the realities of age. Organizers and advisors agreed on five characteristics that have come to distinguish the project.

✦ Age in America is an interdisciplinary initiative, based on the recognition that age, like life itself, does not belong to one academic discipline. The program is intended to rely on such disciplines as literature, art history, philosophy, and the visual arts to frame new approaches to understanding older adults in a variety of historical and cultural contexts.

✦ Age in America is a multi-institutional series of programs that capitalize on the diversity and assets of America's libraries, museums, and historical societies. By offering institutions thematic approaches to the subject of aging and engaging them in a coordinated collaboration, we intended to explore a new approach to decentralized public programming around a topic of contemporary significance.

✦ Age in America emphasizes collaboration—collaboration between the core library and museum partners and collaboration with other community organizations and agencies with complementary missions.

✦ Age in America encourages integration of the "age" theme into ongoing programs, with the goal of demonstrating approaches for incorporating aging as an appropriate theme for public cultural programming.

◆ Age in America draws on contemporary scholarship and in so doing is becoming a bridge between academic and cultural programming practitioners.

Age in America is structured as a national initiative that supports and links local projects or "demonstrations." The local partners are addressing the basic theme of the changing role of the older adult in society through the lens of one or more subthemes: age and aging in the home; age and work; and age in the community. Although each of the projects is unique, they are also similar in notable ways. For example, all three communities are using oral history as a tool to discover local history and to enhance public programs. All have reached out to multigenerational audiences, developing multiplatform programs—effectively treating Age in America as a special exhibition, focused on a central event and supplemented by lectures, discussions, websites, and other social experiences. Each of the communities is offering programs that place local experiences in the context of broader national trends. Most often the national perspective is represented by a lecturing expert, while the local experiences are revealed by photographs, artwork, and other memorabilia.

In each participating community, the partnering institutions are interpreting the topic of Age in America in unique ways that reflect their institutional goals, collections and resources, and audiences. Working collaboratively, these institutions are interpreting age through material culture, art, historical records, images, and oral recordings. In one instance the local process includes the creation of new art inspired by the presenting institutions' collections. They are presenting complementary programs that resonate with and involve their particular local audiences. At the same time, the core partners in the demonstration communities are reaching out to additional partners to broaden discussion of age and aging as a historical and cultural phenomenon. The museum-library teams are building new bridges to other community collaborators, extending the conversation about aging to new venues and new audiences.

CONCLUSION

The longevity revolution is upon us, and it will continue to challenge our long-held beliefs about age and aging. Our popular culture—music, film, television, sports—depicts a world of eternal youth. The few older adults we see on television are generally confined to commercials selling drugs for arthritis, high blood pressure, and other ailments vaguely, and stereotypically, related to age. Moreover, all those adults seem to be living some version of their golden years, retired but still fit—playing golf, traveling, and otherwise engaging in "age-appropriate" activities.

But the reality is different from this stereotype. Both economic need and personal satisfaction keep many older adults in the workplace long after the age of 65. At home, some older adults are raising their grandchildren, while others are downsizing and moving cross-country. In communities nationwide, older adults are volunteering on behalf of the environment, for political candidates, in support of local schools—for myriad social and cultural causes. We need a new set of images, a new way of thinking about age. In short, we need to recognize that *old* is a cultural construct.

Libraries and museums can help us accommodate to our changing demographics. They have adapted their services and facilities to meet the needs of their changing constituents, and they remain trusted institutions in our communities. As the examples in this chapter demonstrate, cultural institutions have the resources and the stature to convene public programs that help explore pressing modern issues.

Libraries and museums also have a tradition of cultural exploration that is critical to understanding the current longevity revolution. We need to invent a new approach to age, and if it is to be effective, it must be an approach that helps us talk across generations, across class and racial lines, across the stereotypes. Only the humanities have the ability to transport us out of our immediate circumstances and frame a new set of paradigms. They introduce us to the past as well as to new ideas. They reveal both old and new images—and they help us imagine new ideas and new relationships. If we can harness the resources of our cultural organizations, we can help our communities negotiate a new set of concepts about and a new set of roles for the older adults among us.

REFERENCES

Achenbaum, A., and P. A. Kusnerz. 1978. Images of old age in America: 1790 to the present. Exhibition and catalog produced by the Institute of Gerontology at the University of Michigan–Wayne State University.

Bateson, M. C. 2008. Interview by Selma Thomas. July. www.ageinamerica.org/Forum .html.

Butler, R. 2008. *The longevity revolution: The benefits and challenges of living a long life.* New York: Public Affairs.

Liroff, S. R., and C. Van Fleet. 1992. Silver Editions II: Humanities programming for older adults. *RQ* 31:473–76.

RECLAIMING THE "PUBLIC" LIBRARY
Engaging Immigrants, Building Democracy

Nan Kari and David Scheie

Deeply embedded in library ethos are the aims to ensure intellectual freedom and individual choice and to provide access to learning for a broad diversity of people. Libraries are among the few openly accessible institutions in our society, but they too are impacted by broad and complex societal trends. In recent decades we have witnessed a dramatic shift in balance between attention to the commons on the one hand and focus on private interests on the other. As we begin the twenty-first century, the values of the free market—too often conflated with the definition of democracy—have infused our societal institutions, many of which have drifted from their founding public missions. This is evident in the pervasiveness of marketplace language—*bottom line, customer choice, service delivery*—all of which help to render citizens consumers rather than productive contributors to our common life. At the turn of the twentieth century and into the 1930s, locally grounded institutions where people could work together to set agendas and address common issues were important democratic spaces. Few remain today. Organizations such as settlement houses, YWCAs, labor unions, and sometimes libraries have shifted from working *with* the public to supplying commodities and delivering services. How to remake and bolster democratic practices within our institutions is an urgent consideration.

Libraries serve communal purposes—as public gathering places and as sources of information relevant to local problem-solving challenges. Branch libraries have long been recognized for their demographic knowledge of the communities in which they are located. To discover the makeup of the neighborhoods they served, many libraries regularly surveyed the local population, businesses, and resources available, often presenting the results in color-coded maps to show relevant patterns (Jones 1999, 15).

Libraries also have an opportunity to promote tolerance and inclusivity through the materials they display—gay and lesbian literature and multicultural and multilingual materials as well as writings by local community members. In so doing, libraries send a strong message that there are many sources of legitimate knowledge. This encompassing approach gives visibility to diverse groups, helps inform the public, and can open new opportunities for relationship building. With the increasing ethnic diversity of our population, libraries have particularly important public roles to play in and with communities.

In this time of economic hardship, people are using library resources in growing numbers. In January 2009, the *Boston Globe,* referring to libraries as "recession sanctuaries," reported:

> Checkouts of books, CDs, and DVDs are up 15 percent at the main library in Modesto, Calif. In Boulder, Colo., circulation of job-hunting materials is up 14 percent. Usage of the Newark Public Library in New Jersey is up 17 percent. Library card requests have increased 27 percent in the last half of 2008 in San Francisco. The Boise Public Library reported a 61 percent increase in new library cards in 2008. In Brantley County, Georgia, library computer usage was up 26 percent in the last quarter. (Jackson 2009)

Yet even as the public's utilization of libraries grows, when cities and counties across the country want to cut budgets, libraries often become targets. Much is at stake for lifelong learners and their communities.

At the largest level, libraries hold the potential to reawaken society's experience of and recommitment to democratic institutions. They offer public spaces where citizens can engage democratic practices. We pose that public libraries are not democratic by default but, rather, through conscious decision of local residents who use them, librarians, and leaders within the profession. The challenge for libraries is, partly, how to combine the free democratic tradition of individual privacy and choice with community-building values that foster connection and interaction among people.

This chapter addresses the democratic possibilities of public libraries and their importance particularly to immigrants, many of whom are lifelong learners. We draw in part from lessons learned at the Jane Addams School for Democracy (JAS), a community-based civic initiative with immigrant families and U.S.-born college students and neighbors located in St. Paul, Minnesota. JAS was conceived and continues as an experiment in democracy that aspires to create and sustain open spaces where diverse people can shape agendas and work together on issues of common concern. We also draw on examples of several libraries that provide models of creative engagement with immigrants.

LIBRARIES AND IMMIGRANTS—A LONG HISTORY

Service among immigrants is a new and fertile field for a life work of usefulness. It is also a national necessity. America has before it the problem of assimilating millions of foreign-born residents, so that Americanization will preserve the best in all peoples for one nation.

— Committee for Immigrants in America, 1916, 3

In the period of open immigration in the United States, from the latter nineteenth century through World War I and until 1924, libraries played a key role in the "Americanization" of newcomers. These efforts to promote cultural enlightenment and "good habits," citizenship and assimilation became part of the early mission of the American public library. Libraries organized English literacy classes; they provided materials for vocational learning and offered information about adult education opportunities outside the library. They often collaborated with other civic organizations such as the YMCA, settlement houses, and labor unions that also promoted citizenship. Libraries distributed books to factories, department stores, and churches—places used by working-class people—and librarians often made home visits to extend their reach to immigrant communities. It was not uncommon for libraries to work with government agencies to educate newcomers. In 1912, for example, the New York Public Library cooperated with the departments of health and child welfare to teach immigrants about health and hygiene (Jones 1999, 10).

Many libraries worked with evening adult education classes to prepare immigrants for citizenship. It was often here that immigrants learned about library services. Libraries also organized nonbook activities such as lectures, performances, and exhibitions of immigrant arts in conjunction with evening classes. Around 1920, these immigrant-focused library activities began to find resonance with the adult education movement. Although a merging of library work with immigrants and the adult education movement was controversial within the library profession, 1924 marked the beginning of the first formal phase of library adult education, which was sustained until the 1930s (Rachal 1989). It should be noted that adult education was intended for the "uplift" of all adults, not only immigrants. This, it was believed, would contribute to the democratic ideal of an educated citizenry.

In these years, libraries across the country built collections of non-English books and papers to serve the interests of immigrant groups in their locale. Recent arrivals as well as citizens seeking connection with their cultural roots used the materials. Although there was debate about the value of offering non-English literature in the Americanization project, historian Plummer Alston Jones notes librarians stood firm. "The majority response from librarians from New York to Minneapolis, based on extensive personal experience with their immigrant patrons, consistently affirmed that the provision of foreign language materials enhanced, rather than hindered Americanization" (Jones 1999, 12).

The political climate in the United States changed after World War I. In response to the Red Scare, immigration laws tightened. Passage of the National Origins Act of 1924 restricted immigration for those outside northwestern Europe and the Western Hemisphere. Jones describes a redoubling of effort on the part of librarians to further Americanization of immigrants, though now with an emphasis on tolerance for diversity (Jones 1999, 21). Bolstered by the progressive philosophy of the Carnegie Corporation, libraries continued their outreach and programs for immigrant patrons but by the end of the decade dropped the term *Americanization*.

LIBRARIES AND IMMIGRANTS—TODAY

Librarians' advocacy for immigrant services and access for all members of the community has continued through the decades to the present. In the spring of 2006 when immigrants' rights groups organized large rallies in Chicago, Los Angeles, and New York to oppose federal legislation aimed at restricting public services to people with documentation, librarians joined with social workers, priests, counselors, and others in support of all immigrants' rights to free public library access. In April 2006, the Association to Promote Library and Information Services to Latinos and the Spanish Speaking (REFORMA) approved a resolution that "encourage[s] library workers to act as advocates for the education of undocumented immigrants about their human rights" (Ascencio 2006). The group also developed the "Librarian's

Toolkit for Responding Effectively to Anti-Immigrant Sentiment" (www.reforma .org/ToolkitPartI.pdf).

Libraries across the country in small towns and large cities offer creative examples of work with new immigrants. The Pelican Rapids Public Library provides one such illustration. Pelican Rapids, a small town settled by people predominantly of European heritage, is located in rural west central Minnesota. In the 1990s, when immigrants and refugees from distant homelands of Somalia, Vietnam, Bosnia, Kurdistan, and Mexico sought employment primarily in food processing, the population of 1,800 people expanded by 700. Not surprisingly, this rapid demographic change challenged the community in multiple ways. The public library—in collaboration with Friends of the Library, townspeople, and several community organizations—has played a central role in facilitating the integration of newcomers and encouraging community dialogue to help foster understanding and acceptance of the changes. A new library building that includes a multicultural learning center was opened in downtown Pelican Rapids in 2003. Its public access computers are used heavily by immigrants to communicate with family and friends in their country of origin. The computers also include English as a New Language (ENL) programs, and the library is a primary site for ENL classes.

In one effort to preserve and make visible immigrant stories, the library initiated a project called The Faces of Change (http://pelicanrapids.lib.mn.us/facesofchange .html). Through photography and oral histories, the project documented the experiences of forty new immigrants and refugees as well as the local residents who helped them. The process of documentation was as important as the final product. It brought new people of all ages into the library, provided occasion for cross-cultural relationships to form, held a mirror for Pelican Rapids to see itself anew, and served to welcome newcomers through recognition of their cultures and individual experiences. The traveling exhibit also became a venue for Pelican Rapids residents to share their community's experience with other towns. The example of the Pelican Rapids Public Library illustrates how libraries can function as community catalysts as well as resource providers.

In 2008 the Urban Libraries Council published a report by Rick Ashton and Danielle Milam on libraries' work with immigrants, called *Welcome, Stranger: Public Libraries Build the Global Village.* Based on surveys of thirty-five libraries in 2007, an earlier survey of seventy-five libraries in 2003, interviews with library and community professionals, and a scan of the literature on immigrant integration, the report concludes that urban libraries make significant contributions to their communities in facilitating immigrant integration. It details five strategies that support successful immigrant transitions and community adaptations that parallel historical activities:

✦ Libraries understand and effectively use local immigration demographics to work with partners and adapt services.

✦ Libraries bring cultural and language sensitivity through signage, multilingual collections, and services.

✦ Libraries build English capacity through literacy-learning opportunities.

✦ Libraries are connecting agencies, linking immigrants with a variety of community services and resources.

◆ Libraries encourage civic engagement by fostering public conversation about issues related to migration and community change. (Ashton and Milam 2008, 5)

Ashton and Milam note libraries' "historic role as strong, unbiased public spaces, dedicated to learning and exploration" (5).

DEMOCRATIC SPACE

Libraries provide public spaces—free, accessible places where diverse people can meet and interact. There are many kinds of public places—airports, schools, parks, open air markets, to name a few. But public places are not necessarily democratic spaces where people can dialogue, engage in public work, cocreate new knowledge, and practice the responsibilities and skills of citizenship. (By *public work* we mean sustained work of value, paid or unpaid, done in public and for purpose. For further discussion of the concept, see Boyte and Kari 1996.)

What constitutes a democratic space? The physical properties of such a space include concrete, visible features that create accessibility—chairs arranged so all can see and participate equally; signage in multiple languages; translators for multilingual groups; artifacts that acknowledge communities that use the space. Equally important but more abstract is the social dimension—elements such as the norms or rules that groups follow; the values reflected in the quality of interactions; and the group's processes, which might include agenda setting, decision making, and evaluation. Implicit are the power dynamics—power understood as coproduced and relational rather than one-way and zero-sum, and power recognized in its multiple forms.

Democratic practices embody a particular set of values shared among those who participate. Peter Moss, who writes about democracy and early childhood education, names the following values as critical: respect for diversity that he describes in terms of "relational ethics"; acknowledgment and integration of multiple worldviews; welcoming of curiosity and ambiguity; and critical thinking or adoption of a critical attitude toward what is commonly accepted as true—a critical element in any democratic society (2007, 18). These values and their related practices are difficult to achieve in part because they contrast markedly with expectations and roles associated with the more familiar service delivery and education models.

The experience of the Jane Addams School for Democracy (JAS) in St. Paul offers several lessons for libraries that wish to become more "public." A central goal of JAS is to create a public space where ordinary people—citizens, refugees, and immigrants; adults and children—learn how to work together to build strong communities. Toward this end, JAS provides an interactive, intergenerational teaching/learning environment. It has become a place rich with both discussions of and active engagement in democratic practices. At JAS, immigrant families develop English language skills, prepare for the citizenship test, strengthen job communication skills, and develop public leadership through ongoing public work to improve human rights and address public issues. Its nonbureaucratic and nonhierarchical, learner-centered philosophy engenders confidence that people can work together to address issues that shape their everyday lives (Kari and Skelton 2007).

Attention to the organizational values and democratic philosophy is essential but not enough. We have seen that citizenship is far more than a legal designation. People need opportunity to engage with each other—through both dialogue and action—on matters of importance to develop identities of productive public people. Productive engagement includes thinking inclusively about multiple sources of knowledge—expert knowledge, knowing from lived experience, new knowledge cocreated through ongoing action and reflection. It requires open, unprogrammed spaces that invite participants to set agendas and engage in a shared discovery learning process. It requires participatory, ongoing evaluation and reflection.

Sustaining a democratic space also requires leadership from people who understand and act on the public dimension of their roles. When experts view their role as "working with" rather than "providing for," such an orientation entails reciprocal and facilitative engagement rather than one-way interactions that can eclipse the knowledge and experiences of participants. Middle Country Public Library in central Long Island, New York, is one place where the librarians have embraced this democratic conception of leadership—while noting that their graduate training in library science gave them little preparation for this viewpoint.

"The process of becoming a 'public' librarian takes time," says Middle Country librarian Sandra Feinberg. "It requires self-assuredness about the role. If you are open, you can think about your role more broadly. Leadership means participating as an equal. This is when you really learn" (Feinberg 2008). The library uses multiple citizen advisory councils to plan and lead activities. Like the Pelican Rapids library, Middle Country partners with museums, the chamber of commerce, other institutions, and residents on both programming and broader community improvement initiatives.

LIBRARIES AND OLDER IMMIGRANTS

Libraries can play vital roles in engagement of older immigrants and refugees. Although children go to school and those of working age head to workplaces where they engage with American language and culture, immigrant elders are more often socially isolated, spending their days behind apartment doors. Libraries are one of the few public spaces where they are welcome.

One challenge in connecting with immigrant elders is that they are more likely to lack literacy in their native language, especially those from developing nations. For them, the opportunity to read native-language newspapers on the library's computers, or check out books in English or other languages, holds little attraction.

English conversation circles are one of the strong draws libraries can offer such elders. In the Minneapolis–Hennepin County Public Library system, for example, conversation circles are popular at many branch libraries where they attract mainly older immigrants. Run by volunteers, coordinated by a library staff person, guided by ENL curricula, the circles offer safe spaces where newcomers can practice their English skills. They also "give people opportunity to talk about their experiences, which is very important," notes senior librarian Deb Reierson of the East Lake branch library in Minneapolis, which has many Somali and Latino patrons (Reierson

2008). Older immigrants, whose life stories include so much resiliency and loss, grief and courage, and who have been challenged to adapt to so many new circumstances, often find such conversation spaces especially valuable.

Hiring immigrants as librarians and library aides helps connect across cultures. The Minneapolis system has its Somali, Latino, Hmong, and other aides engage in off-site outreach activities, too—showing up at immigrant community events and gathering places to explain the library's resources and sign people up for library cards (Reierson 2008).

CONCLUSION

Reinvigoration of our democratic culture requires a recovery of public spaces, open to all. Public space invites connections among people. Public relationships form the heart of a working democracy. Opening and sustaining these spaces, however, is no easy task. This work cannot be accomplished mainly through Internet connections—although the Internet has a unique capacity to build organizing networks. Rather, creating a working democracy requires face-to-face relationship building in real places grounded in real communities. The absence of a sense of grounding in a place is a loss not only for immigrants trying to make a new home but also for native-born citizens. Public spaces owned and used by people in local communities, especially places that commingle immigrants' histories and cultures with the traditions of native-born Americans, can be an extraordinary contribution to revitalization of civic life and democracy.

In an America overtaken by malls and markets, libraries stand out as working examples of free public spaces, a community commons where all can learn and connect and grow. Librarians who choose to embrace this democratic tradition can, through their practices and partnerships, make vital contributions to the reclaiming of common spaces for the common good. They can lead in renewal of community for immigrants and U.S. born, elders and young people alike.

REFERENCES

Ascencio, M. 2006. REFORMA BOD to vote on resolution opposing H.R. 4437. REFORMA Legislative Committee blog, April 12. http://libraryadvocacy.blogspot .com/2006/04/reforma-bod-to-vote-on-resolution.html.

Ashton, R. J., and D. P. Milam. 2008. *Welcome, stranger: Public libraries build the global village.* Chicago: Urban Libraries Council.

Boyte, H., and N. Kari. 1996. *Building America: The democratic possibilities of public work.* Philadelphia: Temple Press.

Committee for Immigrants in America. 1916. *Professional course for service among immigrants: Many peoples one nation America. Manual prepared for the use of colleges and universities, schools of civics and philanthropy, to fit men and women for service among immigrants. Adapted also for study by clubs, institutions and conferences of workers of social organizations.* University of California.

Feinberg, S. 2008. Interview by Nan Kari, David Scheie, and Diantha Schull. August 19. Long Island, New York.

Jackson, D. 2009. The library—A recession sanctuary. *Boston Globe,* January 3.

Jones, P. A. 1999. *Immigrants, libraries, and the American experience.* Westport, CT: Greenwood Press.

Kari, N., and N. Skelton, eds. 2007. *Voices of hope: The story of the Jane Addams School for Democracy.* Dayton, OH: Charles F. Kettering Foundation.

Moss, P. 2007. Bringing politics into the nursery: Early childhood education as a democratic practice. Working paper 43. The Hague, Netherlands: Bernard van Leer Foundation.

Rachal, J. R. 1989. The American library adult education movement: The diffusion of knowledge and the democratic ideal, 1924–1933. In *Breaking new ground: The development of adult and workers' education in North America. Proceedings from the Syracuse University Kellogg Project's First Visiting Scholar Conference in the History of Adult Education,* ed. Rae Wahl Rohfeld, 16–31. Syracuse, NY: Syracuse University. www-distance.syr.edu/rachal.html.

Reierson, D. 2008. Interview by David Scheie. December 10. Minneapolis, Minnesota.

THE LIBRARY AS PLACE IN AN AGING SOCIETY

10

Diantha Dow Schull

*Place is not merely a stage for who we are and what we do,
but integral to life's meaning.*

—Dr. Thomas Dean, Director of the Iowa
Project on Place Studies

What do we know about theories of place, and how can these theories inform libraries as places for positive aging? The answers to these questions are not clear-cut; *place* has multiple meanings. For instance, there is an emerging discipline of Place Studies, defined as the study of "the centrality of natural, built, social, and cultural environments in the formation of individual, group, and communal identity, as well as the ways in which human beings interact with the world" (Dean 2007). Variations on Place Studies include Environmental Sociology and Environment Behavior and Place Studies. These, in turn, break down into specialties such as community and facility design for special populations, the social dimensions of the natural and human environments, and the study of place and landscape.

Although Place Studies may seem outside the realm of library and information science, it offers librarians a way of thinking about the library from an ecological perspective, including how the library interacts with other elements of its environment and what distinguishes it within that environment.

Place as a concept has been appropriated and studied by many types of professionals—urban planners, sociologists, community organizers, economists, developmental psychologists, and architects, to name just a few. For the purposes of this chapter, we examine place along five domains relevant to how the library prepares for an aging society: Symbolic, Community Context, Individual Associations, Experiential, and Spatial (see figure 10.1). We pay particular attention to the first four of these domains. The fifth domain, which involves a range of design issues, merits more detailed exploration than is possible in this publication.

Some might ask whether there is merit in focusing new attention on libraries as physical places, especially for baby boomers, many of whom are avid participants in or even creators of online environments. However, study after study of user preferences and patterns reveals adults' continuing demand for physical venues (Gosling 2000). In a recent survey of Lifelong Access Fellows, a national cadre of librarians trained to focus on active older adults, a high percentage of respondents indicated

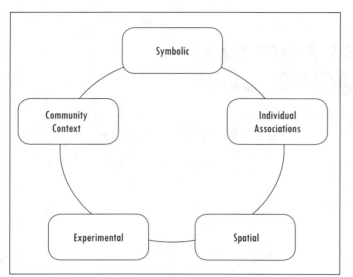

FIGURE 10.1   Place domains: libraries and positive aging

that expansion of meeting and learning spaces was their primary need (Schull 2008). These statistics affirm the views of William Mitchell, noted authority on virtual environments, who explores the future of place in *e-topia* (1999).

> [T]he power of place will prevail. As traditional locational imperatives weaken, we will gravitate to settings that offer particular cultural, scenic and climatic attractions—those unique qualities that cannot be pumped through a wire—together with those face-to-face interactions we care most about.

To fulfill Dr. Mitchell's prophecy, libraries must develop a model for older adult practice that is attentive to the attributes of place.

COMMUNITY CONTEXT DIMENSION

Libraries, as part of the community fabric, can and should be part of the solution.

—Kendall Wiggin, *Coming of Age* (2003)

Our first consideration of the library as place must take into account its position within the larger community. What is the library's relationship to other community entities and educational or service systems? How do these relationships affect older adults' perceptions and experiences of the library as place? To answer these questions we suggest that librarians familiarize themselves with new thinking in a variety of community development topics, all of which are relevant to an aging society.

Access

Examination of the library as a place within a larger place starts with location, an issue that affects library use by all members of a community, not just older adults. Environmental analyst and librarian Christine Koontz (1997) is a leading theorist about library siting: "Location determines the long-term success of the library. . . . Location and site analysis is the first step in offering equitable community-based library services that meet the needs of the unique population served by each facility." Koontz underscores the importance of site analysis to acquire demographic information about local residents and where they reside, how they travel, where they shop, what other destinations and activities draw people to the area, and what changes are anticipated in housing density and demography. By gathering similar data on older adults in their service area, librarians can plan for future facilities or carry out informed changes to current services and facilities to maximize use by older patrons.

Access also implies questions about barriers—physical, transport, service, or cultural barriers—and other issues around what is called *livability*. AARP, a leader in efforts to promote livability, defines a livable community as "one that has affordable and appropriate housing, supportive community features and services, and adequate mobility options, which together facilitate personal independence and the engagement of residents in civic and social life" (AARP 2005).

Access and livability are the focus of many studies and practical initiatives in both the public and private sectors. The state of Arizona has produced *Aging 2020: Arizona's Plan for an Aging Population* to "ensure that Arizona's communities are good places for people of all ages to live with independence, purpose and dignity" (State of Arizona 2005). The University of California's Center for the Advanced Study of Aging Services convened an international online conference in 2007, Creating Aging-Friendly Communities (www.agingfriendly.org). The New York Academy of Medicine, with support from the Mayor's Office and the City Council, recently published findings from a major investigation of how to "adapt our city and our neighborhoods to make sure older adults lead happy, healthy, and productive lives" (New York Academy of Medicine 2008). In the nonprofit sector, Partners for Livable Communities is carrying out an Aging in Place Initiative that focuses on methods "for communities to improve their livability for older persons, and, in turn increase their livability for all people" (www.aginginplaceinitiative.org). The initiative incorporates the term *aging in place,* referring to the trend for people to age in their homes or communities, rather than move to new locations.

These kinds of studies and checklists on access and livability offer useful tools for gauging how an individual library or library system lives up to local standards, where it fits into the local service picture, and what opportunities there may be for the library to fill gaps in positive aging services.

Local Planning

Numerous community planning approaches offer insights regarding the library's relationships to its larger community and how these relationships affect older adult use.

Public space is an important focus for some planners, especially those concerned with planning that affects the library as a civic institution or a commons (Schull 2004). The Project for Public Spaces (PPS) is a leader in documenting and encouraging people-oriented designs for common spaces such as markets, parks, streets, government buildings, and public transportation (www.pps.org). PPS sees the library as an essential component of a community's public infrastructure and has studied libraries in relation to parks (Schull 1998) and as examples of place-making (Schull 2007). Fred Kent, PPS president, calls libraries "the community's front porch."

Relationships between generations are another planning concern with implications for libraries. The Temple University Intergenerational Center, for instance, is promulgating a community planning approach called Communities for All Ages that "focuses on transforming varied age groups and organizations from competitors to allies" (www.templecil.org; www.communitiesforallages.org). As a place that is inherently intergenerational, the library has become a partner in some of the center's demonstration projects.

The Asset-Based Community Development (ABCD) Institute at Northwestern University is yet another organization that defines the library as an essential community place. Its leaders see libraries as a "fulcrum" for community information and a tool for community problem solving and community building (Kretzman and McNight 1993).

Whatever their community's size or location, librarians can inform themselves about how they fit into the larger picture of "places" for healthy aging. By doing so, they not only build their own capacity to work with older adults but also raise planners' and aging specialists' awareness of the roles that libraries can play in the lives of older adults.

Urban Development

The concept of the library as an urban asset and an anchor for urban development has influenced construction of major urban libraries in cities from Denver and Phoenix to Fayetteville and Nashville. A planning document for the Nashville Chamber of Commerce states:

> A city's belief in the value of knowledge as evidence[d] by its support of the public library system is a clear indicator of its overall vitality, as well as its attractiveness to persons and businesses seeking a positive environment in which to do business or to raise a family. (Mattern 2007, 36)

The library's role as a magnet for new residential development, business development, creativity, and social capital takes on special importance in relation to an aging society. Just as those qualities are essential for the vitality of cities, so are they essential for vital aging. Librarians can take advantage of urban planners' new appreciation of the beneficial impacts of libraries as they, in turn, plan for aging services and programs in a supportive community environment.

Richard Florida, author of *The Rise of the Creative Class,* sees libraries as one of the institutions that can help transform a city into a stimulating, diversified, and productive environment. He states, "[F]or society to prosper, it must rely on the creativity and intellect of its people. . . . [L]ibraries and schools are 'creative hubs' that help people increase their creative capability" (2002).

Economic Role

The library as place is sometimes situated within economic planning as an investment that adds direct or indirect value to the local economy. This is a relatively recent approach, driven in part by contemporary demands for greater accountability for public dollars. It has stimulated the nascent field of library valuation, with a spate of more than a dozen studies in the last five years (Americans for Libraries Council 2007). Considering the contributions of older adults to the tax base of a town or city, to its reputation, retail activity, and social capital, it would seem appropriate for researchers to measure the return on investment in places, such as libraries, that help retain or attract age 50+ residents *and* help them participate in community life. Until such data are available, librarians should become familiar with library valuation approaches and consider how they can communicate the economic value of the library as a positive place for older residents.

INDIVIDUAL ASSOCIATIONS DIMENSION

The definition of a heart, to me, is something that keeps a body alive. . . .
[T]his library is a place that keeps the mind and body growing.

—Patron of the T. B. Scott Free Library in Merrill, Wisconsin

As librarians reconsider their services and facilities in an aging society, they will need to examine not only their position in the larger community but also what individuals bring to the library experience. What preconceptions, assumptions, recent experiences, and memories—or lack thereof—do 50+ adults carry with them as they consider whether and how to enter the library space? Do they see the library as a place for individual inquiry, social interchange, inspiration, information, therapy, comfort—none of these or all of these?

The Library as Third Place

The notion of a Third Place, a place that is neither work nor home, is widely understood and referenced; it is also widely associated with the library. Coined by sociologist Ray Oldenburg in 1989, the term is a touchstone for many librarians and library users (Oldenburg 1989). Third Place affirms the importance of the characteristics that meet certain individuals' needs for a neutral, welcoming space: free access; nonjudgmental atmosphere; familiarity; and opportunities for independent, noncommercial activity. All these characteristics are fundamental to the library and can be powerful magnets for older adults, particularly baby boomers, who are known for their independence and penchant for reshaping institutions and cultural practices (Tremain 2002).

Self-Image

For most age groups there is a generally accepted label that helps define who they are—parents, students, teenagers, or Gen Xers. For older adults, this clarity has broken down. *Senior* is no longer adequate or appropriate for the multiple generations of older adults who span more than five decades and whose capacities, interests, and occupations are hugely varied and constantly evolving.

In recent years there has been a gradual transformation of the concept of old age, from senior citizen to "third-ager," or someone who creates her or his own life structures rather than fitting into a particular role or expected behaviors (Gilleard and Higgs 2000). This is a far more open-ended kind of identity—one that raises new questions and new possibilities. There is no longer a consensus about such basics as when one should retire, what one should do in retirement, or whether one should retire at all. People reaching 45 or 55 or 60 are starting to come to grips with the implications of their own longevity; they are recognizing that the length of time between being a full-time parent and worker and being a "frail elder" could be quite long. That recognition poses all sorts of possibilities and requires choices—what some scholars call "the active construction of a 'post-work' identity" (Gilleard and Higgs 2000). Although this task is influenced by values, gender, economic status, cultural traditions, and geographic location, most 50+ adults will at some point, and perhaps at several points, engage in a process of self-examination to determine their options and choices for their next life stage.

During the self-discovery process and during transitions to new life stages, individuals may explore multiple pathways. There is no rule book for older adult transitions, and so the process is fluid and subject to all sorts of influences. Market forces, of course, are a considerable influence, affecting how individuals of all ages, not just adults, perceive and define aging and "retirement" and associated choices. Notwithstanding the variety of influences on their thinking, or perhaps because of them, many individuals recognize the need for information, ideas, and models. They recognize, especially, the importance of trusted information and the value of exposure to peers who are wrestling with similar choices. This is where the library has an enormous opportunity to provide a place—a place for trusted information, assistance, and interaction with peers and others on questions of personal and social transition.

Recognizing the significance of transition to its current and potential older patrons, the New Haven Public Library has developed a Transition Center with collections and programs organized around the needs of adults undergoing life changes (www.cityofnewhaven.com/library/transition.asp).

Although there are other important aspects of self-image, such as the process of "life review" (Butler 2008, 391–92) or of discovering what some call "active wisdom" (see Bateson, chapter 6 in this book), these usually take place within the context of transition. Librarians seeking to understand what identities and life questions older adults bring to the library must understand the importance of transitions and the need to create places and programs that facilitate self-examination, reflection, and self-discovery.

Memories and Local Associations

In characterizing the gains of aging, most researchers would agree that one gain is an "expanding store of memories, experiences and competencies" (Ranzijn 2002). With today's emphasis on productive aging and civic engagement, much attention is paid to accumulated competencies and how they can be applied for social renewal. The realm of memory does not receive equal attention; however, it has particular relevance for the library as place.

Memory offers several opportunities for building on past associations to strengthen current connections to the library place. The first is to identify and leverage individuals' memories of particular libraries. Memories of the spaces, the staff, and even the smell of the books can be powerful influences on adult attitudes. Architect Jeffrey Scherer makes this point in his lectures on Carnegie libraries by reminding people that "baby boomers and other older adults grew up in these buildings" (Sherer 2006). Memory can color people's perceptions of the current library and how it might function in a later phase of adulthood, whether or not they used libraries regularly as mature adults. Tabitha King, a benefactor of the public library in Bangor, Maine, states:

At 13 I began to go to Bangor . . . on a daily basis to attend high school. The Bangor Public Library was convenient to the bus stop. It provided shelter in inclement weather, pull-chain toilets in the basements, and the largest collection of books that I had ever encountered. The wooden card catalog spanned an entire wall, and the cards inside were dog-eared with use. In the children's room was the big dollhouse, and later, my first novel had to do with dollhouses. (Gold 1998)

Librarians can capitalize on the familiarity, comfort, and even ownership that come with these kinds of memories. At the same time, they may be challenged to help former patrons accept the changes that have taken place in "their" libraries, as well as to find ways to build equally strong personal connections with individuals who did not use libraries in their younger years.

Another type of individual association correlates with whether and how a patron feels he or she, or his or her community, is represented in the library. Collections of school yearbooks, architectural renderings, oral recordings, diaries, and images of sports teams and community celebrations can be magnets for adult constituencies, especially older patrons. Records, objects, and images that are recognizable and meaningful can transform the library from just another public place into a source of social and individual identity.

A third approach for building connections through memories is to invite older patrons to help create the library of the future, to donate their memories, images, and records or to interpret existing collections through their personal knowledge of people and places. The popularity of such outreach/collection development projects as Shades of L.A. (El Guindi 1996), Reading America (developed by Libraries for the Future), or the national Veterans History Project (www.loc.gov/vets/) reflect the enthusiasm of people invited to make personal contributions to the library.

Librarians confront special challenges in building connections with older adult immigrants, many of whom are from countries without libraries or without public libraries. Some newcomers may associate the library with unpleasant or invasive government practices and may hesitate to explore the physical place. In addition, many older newcomers do not have the linguistic skills or cultural familiarities that enable them to venture into a new space—especially older immigrant women. Librarians must give particular attention to these barriers as they rethink their work with and for older adults.

EXPERIENTIAL DIMENSION

As aging baby boomers make the transition to retirement, they need
sources for life direction and social connections.

—Marc Freedman, November 2003

Past experience with a particular library or perceptions about today's libraries can determine whether and how older adults will approach the library as a place. Once they encounter the library, however, these attitudes can be reaffirmed or reshaped by the quality of the library experience and how it meets users' needs.

Library literature is full of observations and analyses of functional uses of libraries—use of computers and self-checkout machines; use of specific collections, databases, or media; use of quiet areas or commons or parking lots. However, the factors that drive people to make use of these library resources—their developmental needs and personal motivations—are not emphasized in library literature. Even discussions of such terms as the *experience library* or the *learning library* (Selling the learning experience 2003) emphasize *how* the library is used rather than *why*.

Given the diversity of older adults, it is impossible to characterize all their interests and needs. Following are five types of experiences that reflect common needs of 50+ adults and offer opportunities for libraries to become responsive, meaningful places.

Social Experiences

Many librarians understand the value of the library as a commons and a space for group exchange. This function has been recognized especially in relation to the developmental needs of teenagers, with the result that more and more libraries have separate spaces where teens can control their own activities and noise levels. However, there is now equally compelling evidence from gerontologists and other specialists on aging about older adults' needs for and benefits from social connections. New research reveals the strong emotional and even physiological benefits from reducing isolation, maintaining a dense network of social relations, and carrying on regular individual and group communications (Rook, Charles, and Hechausen 2006). The research shows that the health of older adults, their outlook, and their quality of life are enhanced through opportunities for social interaction, whether formal or informal. There is also growing evidence that psychological health, and to some extent physical health, depends at least in some degree on feeling integrated with a community (Hao 2008).

Librarians can confirm the validity of this evidence based on their own observations of older patrons. Adult services specialists interviewed by the author note that older people seem to gravitate toward group settings, take advantage of conversation areas and coffee shops, and seek out peer exchange, contact with younger people, or social networking on the Internet. In a 2008 survey of Lifelong Access librarians, 96 percent of respondents stated that additional physical space for social connections was the primary need of their older adult constituents. Space for group learning was the second-largest need indicated (Schull 2008). These findings underscore the need for all librarians to become aware of the social needs of older adults and to factor these needs into their planning for programs and facilities.

The success of the Connections Café at the Tempe Public Library in Phoenix, Arizona, provides strong evidence of the positive response by older adults to a gathering place that is accessible, stimulating, and conveniently located near information and activities that facilitate community participation. The café is part of Tempe Connections, a special library-based, community initiative that "provides a comprehensive one-stop resource to connect boomers and other young seniors with the information, services, and programs they need to remain informed, engaged, and happy members of the community." The café has an attached programming space where older adults can meet friends, engage in lively discussions, view art displays, listen to music on the outdoor patio, attend a lecture about a topic of interest, and seek out volunteering opportunities (www.tempeconnections.org).

Educational Experiences

With the increasing pace of technological, economic, and cultural change, continuous learning has become an imperative for everyone, no matter his or her age, social status, or formal educational background. One result is the development of a "learning society" (Martin 2004). Another is the explosion of formal and informal learning opportunities for midlife and older adults. From community colleges to elite universities, enrollment is expanding or special programs are evolving for local residents, alumni, and other mature adults (see, e.g., www.swarthmore.edu/lifelong learning.xml).

For some older adults, learning is a necessity for economic security, causing people to continue working beyond prior expectations, gain new skills, or take on new professional challenges. However, research shows that there are other motivations for older adult learning beyond the tangible benefits of improving one's marketable skills. These include the desire to understand the changing environment, satisfy personal curiosities, accomplish long-postponed learning goals, or participate with others in a process of discovery (Moody 2002). Ron Manheimer, director of the North Carolina Center for Creative Retirement, states, "From my limited vantage point, what I see in the people coming and going from the Reuter Center is a desire to be part of a community that has, as its underlying affinity, a love of continued learning" (2008, 182).

Considerable scholarship has been devoted to the motivational factors for older adult learning, and numerous applications of this knowledge exist in both for-profit and nonprofit settings. The success of Elderhostel is not an isolated example. Campus-based institutes for learning in retirement, special degree programs at colleges and universities, courses offered in retirement communities and senior centers, and peer-led learning through the Osher Lifelong Learning Institutes are all part of larger trends.

New research on aging proves that these trends are not just a function of a particular time or social fad but are rooted in physiological and mental needs that are only now beginning to be understood. Although there is no evidence that natural declines or changes in cognitive development can be reversed, there is evidence that with certain behaviors, including continued and regular intellectual stimulation, the timing and scope of these changes can be modified (Lachman 2004). In addition, new research documents older adults' capacities to acquire new skills and to draw on their experience to enhance learning in new areas (Nussbaum 2006).

There are considerable implications of this research for the library's identity as a place for older adult learners. Fortunately, libraries have always seen themselves in one way or another as being in the education or knowledge business. The public library, after all, is considered "the people's university." There is now an opportunity to put real shape and form to that role by strengthening the quality, variety, and regularity of learning experiences for older adult learners and communicating these as flagship programs of the local library.

Transitional Experiences

Just as young people seeking information and counseling on jobs, education, careers, and other life choices turn to libraries, so might older adults undergoing comparable transitions—if the library were clearly positioned as a "transition place."

Research on midlife adults nearing the traditional age of retirement, baby boomers deciding whether to retire and what to do next, and older adults moving from full-time to part-time work or from work to service—or back again—points to the need for information and assistance with transitions (Imel 2003).

Some librarians might say that the normal information resources at the library are adequate to address questions about life transitions. However, when people are facing life changes, new responsibilities, and personal and professional losses, information alone is not enough. From the earlier discussion of self-image and transitions, it should be clear that people in transition require not just data but a human and social place.

Models for transition support are emerging, some of which have relevance for libraries. Next Chapter sites, developed initially by the national organization Civic Ventures, are "accessible community settings that provide information and guidance for life transitions and offers interaction with peers" (Civic Ventures 2005). Next Chapter projects are in different stages of development around the country and consist of collaborative networks of service organizations, educational institutions, and peer-led activities that take place at multiple locations, including libraries. In Chandler, Arizona, for instance, the library is a primary partner in the Boomerang project, a community collaborative designed "to help Boomers and near or recent retirees figure it out" (www.myboomerang.org).

The Discovering What's Next (DWN) project, based at the public library in Newton, Massachusetts, is one of the first and most developed models for a transition place. It is dedicated to "engaging mid-life and older adults in the creative exploration of their next life stage" (www.discoveringwhatsnext.com). DWN was not developed by the library in Newton; local organizers discovered the value of the library as a peer networking place and a gateway to "what's next."

Early in its development, DWN learned that participants were seeking neutral, accessible locations for guidance and for conversations. According to founder Carol Greenfield, organizers explored several different community locations as venues for presentations, information, and dialogue. They determined that

> the public library provided the right balance of public and private for bringing people together who shared a common bond of transition but may not have known each other previously. . . . Because of its centrality to all communities, its non-ageist identification and its vast resources for exploration and discovery, the library is a perfect gateway for this demographic. (Greenfield 2009)

DWN now has established its base of operations in an identifiable separate space at the library and offers varied programs in the library's auditoriums and public spaces. The project offers an instructive example of a community-based effort, now lodged in a welcoming library.

Informational Experiences

Given librarians' expertise in reference services and information-seeking behavior and libraries' fundamental identity as information places, this chapter will not go into detail on ways that libraries could strengthen that identity with older adults. Suffice it to say that, to date, library literature is more focused on information-seeking processes relating to older adults, such as website design and use of the Internet for self-care and health support, than on the content of the information they are seeking. Aside from health, there has been little in-depth investigation of the kinds of information useful for different stages of older adulthood and how access to that information might support positive aging.

The literature on aging and changes taking place in other community institutions can shed light on these issues, providing evidence that demand for certain topics and themes is likely to increase with the increase in numbers of older adults. These topics include work, health and fitness, community service, financial planning, caregiving, spirituality, and, as noted, life transitions. By providing information and services around these topics and by communicating the existence of these services to current and potential patrons, librarians are likely to find that older adults begin to turn to the library for their information needs. Further, by offering programs that complement printed and online information, such as workshops, dialogues, in-person presentations, and one-to-one counseling, the library will be seen not just as a passive information resource but as an experience library, a library that older adults may call *the* information place.

Cultural Experiences

Discussions of the library as place often neglect the cultural experiences available at most libraries, experiences that include exposure to the arts as well as opportunities for participation and creativity. This neglect is surprising, given the popularity of cultural offerings and the increase in demand for cultural experiences that are free, diverse, and accessible. In fact, library space for "forum functions" has increased in recent years, and libraries both large and small assume that cultural activities are part of core services.

The library's tradition as a place for culture is an advantage in terms of attracting older adults, many of whom seek out convenient cultural opportunities. This tradition also underscores the extent to which the library can support positive aging. Recent research by Dr. Gene Cohen, working with the Center for Creative Aging, documents the positive changes that derive from older adults' regular participation in creative and artistic activities (Cohen 2006). Cultural participation can take many forms, from memoir writing workshops and musical performances to poetry festivals and intergenerational theater. For librarians, the challenge is to use spaces and shape activities that enhance cultural appreciation by older adults *as well as* encourage individual and group expression.

SPATIAL DIMENSION

No discussion of the library as place can ignore issues of space and the many questions it engenders in the context of an aging society. All librarians seeking to strengthen the library's position as a place for positive aging will want to examine the library environment in accordance with current theories about how environments can promote well-being, learning, reflection, and participation. These matters go beyond the problems of access discussed earlier; they raise such issues as separate spaces versus age-integrated spaces, comfort and quiet versus stimulation, design of workstations and chairs, aesthetics, and a host of others.

Although library planners and architects have certainly addressed some of these issues, there are numerous other professionals whose perspectives could be useful to the library community. They include gerontologists who specialize in therapeutic environments and architectural planning, designers of adult learning environments, and specialists in the design of work spaces for different age groups. The recent publication *Environment and Identity in Later Life,* which explores "how environmental complexity influences people in developing and maintaining their own identity," is just one of many from other fields that offer insights about spaces for positive aging (Kellaher, Holland, and Peace 2005).

Changes in the design of other educational and service spaces can also be instructive for librarians as they consider the look or feel of libraries in the age of longevity. The Mather Cafés in Chicago offer a new model for senior centers, emphasizing spaces for social connections and other forms of community participation (www .matherlifeways.com/iyc_inyourcommunity.asp). The Osher Lifelong Learning Institute at the University of Maine recently renovated classroom spaces for its older adult students. Kali Lightfoot, director of the national Osher Institutes network and who supervised the changes, observes, "The really important matters were the small things, details such as whether or not the white boards should be glossy or matte, where to place parking, the type of lighting and the shape of the classroom chairs" (Lightfoot 2009).

A serious exploration of space issues cannot be undertaken here. However, some fundamental considerations provide a starting point for librarians to use in analyzing their libraries as places for positive aging. These factors include light, flexibility, amenities, aesthetics, access, and integration. Examining these aspects of the library—even a small and under-resourced library—in relation to the experiential, individual, and symbolic issues discussed in this chapter, will stimulate new ideas about how the library can start to redevelop its physical environment as a place for positive aging.

SYMBOLIC VALUE

The new Main Library in Salt Lake City embodies the idea that a library is more than a repository of books and computers—it engages the city's imagination and aspirations.

—The City Library: The Salt Lake City Library System (2003)

Beyond the community, individual, experiential, and spatial dimensions that shape the library as place, there is yet another dimension that may be the most powerful of all—namely, the library's symbolic value. Hard to capture in words and numbers, this domain takes different forms for different individuals and groups. Library literature is rife with statements attesting to the ways in which the library as place has meaning over and above the library as a source of information and services.

The strength of these symbolic associations helps explain the striking finding about public attitudes toward libraries in the recent national study *Long Overdue*. Researchers found that 78 percent of the individuals sampled, when asked their reaction "if your public library were to shut down tomorrow," stated that they felt it "would be an important loss that affects the whole community." Even people who rarely or never use libraries support raising taxes over other money-saving measures such as reducing services (Public Agenda 2006).

What are some specific values people ascribe to the library as an "essential" community institution? First, it is a place that represents the community. It is a symbol and an identifier, described variously as a cultural icon, a historical marker, or an aesthetic and public asset that expresses the character of the community. Like a lighthouse, it orients people as well as providing a sense of safety and familiarity.

Second, some individuals ascribe qualities to the library that are almost spiritual, expressing sensations of being transported beyond the daily or secular realm to transcendent space. In "A Writer's View: Journey to a Sacred Place," Ethelbert Miller (2006) states:

> During the '50s, when I was growing up in the South Bronx, I thought a trip to the library was a journey to a sacred place. I fell in love with books even before I enjoyed playing baseball. My mother claims she often left my brother, sister, and me at the Hunts Point's Library when she went to the supermarket. If that's true, it might explain why my mind grew more than my body. . . . The public library was a place my parents considered to be just as important as the church. I guess my soul was saved by my introduction to good books.

Third, the library is often described as embodying various ideals held in common by a particular community, group, or individual. One ideal is the concept of public space as a principle for an enlightened and equitable society. This ideal promotes practices that emphasize the library as a commons—a concept that is increasingly reflected in the design and use of academic libraries as well as contemporary public libraries (Steiner and Holley 2009). The other ideal derives from the notion of the library as an instrument and symbol of democratic participation.

> A democracy needs safe gathering places where community members can share interests and concerns. . . . [E]ffective citizen action is possible only when citizens know how to gain access to information . . . and have the skills to become responsible, informed participants in our democracy. (Kranich 2000)

These ideals are part of the library's attraction for older adults, many of whom care deeply about local applications of democratic principles and welcome the chance to be associated with others in a larger symbolic enterprise. The literature on aging tells us that "meaning" is important to older adults—meaning in both a societal sense and in terms of individual identity. It could be argued that the symbolic meaning of the library place may be one of its most powerful dimensions in an aging society.

CONCLUSION

In the future, people may not need to come to the library for information.
They will come in droves if they perceive it as a desirable place.
　　　　　　　　—Fred Kent, "How to Become a Great Public Space"

Libraries have undergone profound changes in the last three decades, and it is likely that they will undergo equally profound changes in the next three decades. Just as the organizational culture of the library has shifted in response to new technologies, new media, and new approaches to scholarship, publishing, and learning, so libraries will continue to evolve. This time, the changes will constitute a response to larger numbers of older adults and the increase in the human life span. These changes will reveal libraries' inherent capacities to become special places for active older adults.

What is exciting and different about these changes is the extent to which they will be informed not by an exclusive "library" mind-set, but by insights and research from other professions and disciplines. In opening up a new chapter of adult services focused on positive aging, more and more libraries will be positioning themselves as valued places for a growing number of community residents. In this respect, they will once again be demonstrating their capacity to evolve as places that enrich the lives of people across the life span.

REFERENCES

AARP. 2005. Liveable communities: An evaluation guide. www.aarp.org/research/ppi/liv-com/Other/articles/livable_communities__an_evaluation_guide.html.

Americans for Libraries Council. 2007. *Worth their weight: An assessment of the evolving field of library valuation.* Available at www.ala.org/ala/research/librarystats/worththeir weight.pdf.

Butler, R. 2008. *The longevity revolution: The benefits and challenges of living a long life.* New York: Public Affairs.

Civic Ventures. 2005. *Blueprint for The Next Chapter.* www.civicventures.org/publications/booklets/blueprint.cfm.

Cohen, G. 2006. *The creativity and aging study: Final report.* George Washington University Center on Aging, Health and Humanities in collaboration with Elders Share the Arts, Centers for Elders and Youth in the Arts, and the Levine School of Music. April.

Coming of age: Building healthy communities in Connecticut. 2003. Unpublished report on a statewide forum presented by Libraries for the Future with the Connecticut State Library. November.

Dean, T. 2007. Changing places: Honoring our past, moving into the future. *University of Iowa Spectator* (Fall): 10.

El Guindi, F. 1996. "Shades of Los Angeles" project spotlights Middle Eastern communities. *Washington Report on Middle East Affairs* (May/June): 61, 104. www.wrmea.com/backissues/0596/9605061.htm.

Florida, R. 2002. *The rise of the creative class.* New York: Basic Books.

Gilleard, C., and P. Higgs. 2000. *Cultures of ageing: Self, citizen and the body.* Upper Saddle River, NJ: Prentice Hall.

Gold, D. 1998. Bangor basks in grandeur of its library. *Boston Globe,* April 12.

Gosling, W. A. 2000. To go or not to go? Library as place. *American Libraries* (December): 44–45.

Greenfield, C. 2009. Interview by Diantha D. Schull. February.

Hao, Y. 2008. Productive activities and psychological well-being among older adults. *Journals of Gerontology,* Series B: Psychological Sciences and Social Sciences 63:S64–S72.

Imel, S. 2003. *Career development of older adults.* ERIC Clearinghouse on Adult Career and Vocational Education. www.ericdigests.org/2005-1/older.htm.

Kellaher, L., C. Holland, and S. M. Peace. 2005. *Environment and identity in later life.* New York: Open University Press.

Koontz, C. M. 1997. *Library facility siting and location handbook.* Westport, CT: Greenwood Press.

Kranich, N. 2000. Libraries as civic spaces. *American Libraries* (November): 7.

Kretzman, J. P., and J. L. McNight. 1993. *Building communities from the inside out: A path toward finding and mobilizing a community's assets.* Asset-Based Community Development Institute of the Institute for Policy Research, Northwestern University.

Lachman, M. E. 2004. Development in midlife. *Annual Review of Psychology* 55:305–31.

Lightfoot, K. 2009. Interview by Diantha D. Schull. February.

Manheimer, R. 2008. Becoming historical to oneself. *Journal of Aging Studies* 22:177–83.

Martin, R. 2004. Libraries and learning. *Advances in librarianship* 28:83–93.

Mattern, S. 2007. *Designing with communities: The new downtown library.* Minneapolis: University of Minnesota Press.

Miller, E. E. 2006. A writer's view: Journey to a sacred place. *American Libraries* 31 (6): 67–68.

Mitchell, W. 1999. *e-topia: "Urban life, Jim—but not as we know it."* Cambridge, MA: MIT Press.

Moody, H. R. 2002. Structure and agency in late-life learning. www.hrmoody.com/articlestext.html.

New York Academy of Medicine. 2008. *Toward an age-friendly New York City: A findings report,* 10. www.nyam.org/initiatives/docs/AgeFriendly.pdf.

Nussbaum, P. 2006. *Brain health and wellness.* Libraries for the Future's Lifelong Access Libraries Leadership Institute. Unpublished presentation. July.

Oldenburg, R. 1989. *The great good place: Cafes, coffee shops, community centers, beauty parlors, general stores, bars, hangouts, and how they get you through the day.* St. Paul, MN: Paragon House (Marlowe 1994).

Public Agenda, with Americans for Libraries Council. 2006. *Long overdue: A fresh look at public and leadership attitudes about libraries in the 21st century.* 2006. www.public agenda.org/files/pdf/Long_Overdue.pdf.

Ranzijn, R. 2002. The potential of older adults to enhance community quality of life: Links between positive psychology and productive aging. *Ageing International* 27 (2).

Rook, K. S., S. T. Charles, and J. H. Hechausen. 2006. Aging and health. In *Foundations of health psychology,* ed. H. Friedman and R. C. Silver. New York: Oxford University Press.

Scherer, J. 2006. *Space planning for social connections.* Presentation at Libraries for the Future's Lifelong Access Libraries National Leadership Institute. July.

Schull, D. D. 1998. Parks and libraries in partnership. *Great parks/great cities, Seattle 1998.* Report on a Leadership Forum on Urban Parks. October. www.pps.org/topics/pubpriv/whybuild/schull/.

———. 2004. The civic library: A model for 21st century participation. *Advances in Librarianship* 28:55–81.

———. 2007. Libraries and placemaking: Libraries are the new commons for the 21st century. *Making places: News and ideas from Project for Public Spaces.* Spring. www.pps.org/info/newsletter/april2007/library_placemaking/.

———. 2008. National Survey of Lifelong Access Libraries: Space and Place for 50+ Adults. Unpublished. December.

Selling the learning experience—Waynn Pearson. 2003. Staff review of Cerritos (CA) Library. *Library Journal,* March 15. www.libraryjournal.com/article/CA281685.html.

State of Arizona, Office of the Governor. 2005. Introduction. In *Aging 2020: Arizona's Plan for an Aging Population.* http://azgovernor.gov/Aging/Documents/Aging2020 Report.pdf.

Steiner, H., and R. P. Holley. 2009. The past, present, and possibilities of commons in the academic library. *Reference Librarian* 50 (4): 309–32.

Tremain, K. 2002. *Where will all the boomers go? The postwar generations' retirement offers opportunities to marry innovations in social and physical neighborhood design.* Report prepared for Civic Ventures. www.civicventures.org/publications/articles/where_will _all_the_boomers_go.cfm.

PART THREE

LIBRARIANS' PERSPECTIVES

CONVERSATIONS AND THE TRUE KNOWLEDGE OF GENERATIONS | 11

R. David Lankes with assistance from Pamela H. Jureller

THE OBLIGATION OF THE LIBRARY

A library has many functions in a community: it entertains, it convenes, it collects, and so on. However, at the heart of any library is a mission to improve the knowledge of its community. In this way libraries are aspirational institutions: they represent what a community wants to be. Libraries in academic, public, school, and special settings represent learning and knowledge.

For this chapter we will focus on the role of the library in enhancing the knowledge of its community by tapping into the considerable knowledge of active older Americans. This age cohort embodies not only a set of expertise but a rich history of applying knowledge to key decisions. As Chaffin and Harlow (2005) note, "Older Americans are typically self-sufficient and self-reliant as a result of their life experiences and the history of their times." Over the past century, life expectancy has increased dramatically (CDC 2007), producing a cohort over age 60 (an arbitrary number) with more life experience than any previous generation. Put simply, today's active older Americans have learned more and applied this learning to more situations than has any previous generation. The library has an obligation to tap into this new national asset.

THE PROBLEMS OF KNOWLEDGE MANAGEMENT

At an ASIS&T (American Society for Information Science and Technology) conference in 2002, IBM scientist David Snowden described a knowledge management system the company had that didn't work. Each worker was expected to write an essay or article that described what she or he knew—the individual's area of expertise. Other workers could then use the system to identify collaborators or other experts within IBM having the needed expertise for a given project. The system didn't work. It didn't work because the articles were lifeless and because it was hard to match a real situation to a static article. The knowledge resided in the heads of the workers, and no essay could capture that dynamic reality.

Similarly, active older Americans have experience and knowledge that are essential to capture and, more important, to apply to current projects and situations. The IBM example shows us one way to capture knowledge that doesn't work but raises an obvious question—how do we transfer knowledge? To answer this question, we must first define our terms. Let's start with *knowledge.*

Gordon Pask set out to define this very word. In the 1960s, he was attempting to teach machines to think and was modeling the behavior of humans learning a task (Pask 1976). What he found, and later codified in Conversation Theory, was that people learn, and know, through conversations. Sometimes these conversations are between two people or between groups. Sometimes these conversations are within a single individual. Researchers call this *metacognition,* or critical thinking. Central to this chapter, conversations can be between different generations.

Of course the definition of *knowledge* requires defining *conversation.* In Conversation Theory, a conversation consists of conversants, language exchanged between the agents, agreements reached by the agents, and a memory that relates and keeps track of all the agreements. It is worth spending some time on these elements of a conversation.

Conversants

Conversants are agents capable of processing and generating information. As previously stated they may be individuals or groups (organizations, societies, generations). An older library patron might be a conversant, or he or she might be part of a conversant when the library is having a cross-generational conversation.

Language

What are these conversants doing in the conversation? They are exchanging language. This language may be very directional and simplistic or very complex. Conversation Theory talks about two levels of language—L0 and L1. L0 language is simplistic. It is exchanged between parties when at least one member of the conversation doesn't know much about the topic. Think about when you are learning something brand new or conducting a reference interview with a patron who knows little about a topic. The language centers on simplistic orienting: "Where do I find information on X?" or "How do I search for Y?" L1 language, on the other hand, takes place between informed conversants. Here the language exchanged is full of shortcuts and specialized terms. The content of the language is probing, unlike the more procedural language of L0. So when two librarians are talking, one might say, "We really should do tagging in the catalog." Outside the library world, however, where catalogs are more about buying things than finding things, this sentence may well be interpreted as adding price tags into a toy catalog.

Language is an important consideration for libraries serving older Americans. These patrons have their own L1, and when engaging them or facilitating cross-generational conversations (as will be discussed later), we must pay attention to normalizing language to prevent frustration and misunderstanding.

Let us be clear, however, that the definitions of L0 and L1 and, indeed, the normalized language used are particular to any given conversation. The attempt should not be to create some general-purpose dictionary of slang but, rather, to assist the parties in any given conversation in making their meanings clear.

Agreements

So why are these conversants exchanging language? They are seeking agreements. Agreements are shared understandings that form the basis of knowing a topic. These agreements are then cobbled together to form even larger understandings of a given domain. Let us return to the question of language and the use of the word *catalog*. A reference librarian might tell a patron to look something up in the catalog. In response to a quizzical look, the librarian might then explain that a catalog is a system that keeps track of all the materials in the library's collection. Once the patron and librarian agree that a catalog in the context of the given conversation is a library system, the librarian can proceed to explain how to effectively use the catalog. The agreement on the meaning of the word *catalog* is necessary to complete the conversation.

Agreements have another important aspect. Although they are initially linked to conversants (who you were talking to when you reached the agreement) and possibly to some artifact (which book I read something in), the agreement tends to merge both conversant and artifact. Thus, after some time, you "know" something, but you aren't sure where you know it from. It is also important to note that although an agreement may have been generated from some artifact like a book, the agreement was reached through a conversation not with the book, but with oneself ("What is the author trying to say?" "How does this fit with what I already know?" "That is an interesting point I will have to remember."). Knowledge can never be encoded and exist outside an individual. Books, web pages, CDs—all these are artifacts that can stimulate knowledge, not house it.

Memory

In order for agreements to scaffold, there must be a memory of the agreement. Although this is hardly surprising, it is important to know that a memory is a relational thing. Agreements are stored not as independent facts, but in relation to one another. This explains the issue of a patron not understanding the concept of a library catalog. The patron knows what a *catalog* is; she or he has simply related the concept of *catalog* to shopping, not inventory. Through the conversation with a librarian, a new connection is made (not necessarily replacing the old concept).

Many knowledge management approaches focus on memory. Yet many of these approaches do not consider that true knowledge is a dynamic and applied process, nor that even the agreements in memory may have little value outside their connection to a much larger and related network of ideas. This means that as libraries seek to engage the knowledge of active older Americans, they must do so in a dynamic and applied way that accounts for the context of knowledge.

PARTICIPATORY LIBRARIANSHIP

Participatory librarianship combines this core theory about knowledge acquisition with the facilitating role of librarians to redefine library functions and services.

Librarians facilitate knowledge by providing *access* to conversations, the *knowledge* necessary to participate in the conversation, a safe *environment* in which to pursue knowledge, and *motivation* for the pursuit.

This participatory approach represents a marked departure from previous knowledge management practice and, indeed, from traditional library approaches. The traditional approach represents a documentcentric view of the world—that is, the belief that knowledge is easily encoded into objects, such as books or videos. The main task of a library in such a documentcentric view is to provide access. To transfer knowledge, one must simply provide access to the right materials. To make access to information effective and efficient, one organizes the information, centralizes access points, and so on. This sort of itemcentric logic explains the dominance of classification and collection in libraries. It also represents a lot of current library service to older patrons. To serve older patrons, build a collection of materials relevant to them (health care books, pointers to web pages on traveling, etc.).

The limitations of the traditional documentcentric approach became evident in IBM's knowledge management system mentioned earlier. Experts didn't transfer their expertise into the system; they created a document. To be clear, documents are not unimportant. After all, if they were seen as having little value, this chapter would not have been written and would not be read. The point is simply that documents are not knowledge. The best they can do is to stimulate a conversation whereby knowledge is gained. By reading this document, you are engaged in a conversation— not with the author, but with yourself. You are attempting to assimilate ideas and facts into your own knowledge. If you are unable to do so, say, because of unusual terminology, you may seek to include additional conversants in the conversation (say, a professor or colleague). Ultimately the IBM system failed because it wanted to capture knowledge but instead captured only documents.

Let us return to the question of capturing knowledge with the participatory librarianship lens in place. If we want to capture the knowledge of active older Americans, we must engage them in conversation. Libraries must facilitate this conversation, both by supporting existing conversations and by designing forums for new conversations with the explicit purpose of transferring knowledge across generational lines. Think of the process as a sort of checklist for new services (see table 11.1).

SUPPORTING THE CONVERSATIONS OF ACTIVE OLDER AMERICANS

One of the basic tenets of participatory librarianship is to be where the conversations are. This means that rather than waiting until someone realizes she needs the library or marketing to potential users, librarians must actively identify and go to the conversation. This means engaging with active older Americans in their social circles, partnering with institutions serving older Americans, and increasing online offerings to those over 65, who are increasingly wired (www.pewinternet.org/topics/Seniors.aspx).

Rather than making a haphazard effort, libraries must deliberately embark on identifying, or mapping, existing conversations. You can begin by identifying major

TABLE 11.1   Checklist for New Services

ELEMENT TO CONSIDER	QUESTIONS TO ASK	POSSIBLE ANSWERS
Elements from Conversation Theory		
Conversants	Who is and should be participating in this conversation? What are the demographics of the targeted service population?	Veterans Retirees Older Americans Grandparents
Language	What terms are commonly used by this population? What are the associated meanings of these terms? What language is needed to accomplish/participate in this service?	Avoid the term *seniors*. The patron must understand basic computer terminology.
Agreements	What are the intended understandings coming into this program? What are the anticipated understandings coming out of this program? What is common wisdom on this topic?	These questions really form the bulk of an assessment plan.
Memory	What is already known about this topic? What are the different perspectives in the literature on this topic?	Pathfinders and annotated bibliographies Oral histories
Elements from Participatory Librarianship		
Access	What are the necessary technologies needed to access this conversation?	Screen readers Blogs Meeting rooms
Knowledge	What do participants need to know in order to learn from this program?	Basic computer literacy Milestones in the conversation over time
Environment	What policies need to be put in place to help people feel comfortable in participating?	Netiquette guidelines for civil conversations A trusted moderator in face-to-face conversations
Motivation	Why would patrons want to engage in this service/ conversation? What is their internal motivation for learning? What external features could be used to motivate patrons to participate?	Money and prizes Awards and recognition Identify hot topics already being discussed by active older Americans

topics being discussed by your older patrons. Although there are sure to be overlaps with national trends, the nature of conversations will be different in every community. For example, academic libraries are increasing their efforts to extend educational offerings and create new forms of lifelong learning engagement with active older Americans. In these communities, the focus might be on building cohorts of older learners around a given curriculum. In some municipalities, the focus of the conversation might be on attracting younger citizens to the area or to public service. In the corporate world, the focus of conversations might be on succession planning. Rather than assuming the nature of the conversations, libraries must see what conversations exist and create service plans around them.

Once the conversation is identified, libraries should determine regularities in the conversation. Regularities can include established steps whereby the conversants gain knowledge. Say, for example, the conversation centers on health insurance options. Is there a process for determining health care options? The point is not to simply toss information at the conversants, but to provide the right support at the right time. If there is an established process, the library should support it—in essence, create curriculums, not collections.

Once the conversation has been mapped, the library can identify useful services. Some services may be information oriented, such as a collection of materials. Other services might provide infrastructure to the conversation. For example, the library might be a meeting place, or it might house materials generated by the conversation itself. The library can also provide vital technical infrastructure that expands the conversation beyond physical place, such as to a wiki, blog, or discussion group. Active older Americans can learn about the importance of computers, the Web, and library physical and cyber accessibility when libraries and community partners design education for that age group (Mates 2004).

A COMING OF AGE EXAMPLE

It is helpful to explore this approach through an example. Pennsylvania is one of a handful of states that skews strongly toward older Americans (Himes 2003). The Free Library of Philadelphia was interested in reaching out to older patrons in its service area, as this demographic also represents active library users. Here is a group of active older Americans seeking both mutual support and some means of preserving their knowledge. In a documentcentric approach, the goal might be twofold: provide the patrons with materials they may need, and gather their materials to build a collection. After all, these active older Americans have a great deal of material about major historical milestones. The library could easily digitize their photographs, letters, and even oral histories. Once in the "create a digital library" mode, the process and technologies practically trip off the tongue: first identify materials for digitization, then develop a taxonomy to describe the terms, next apply Dublin Core metadata, and finally put it all online.

Most older Americans, however, wouldn't identify their issues as a "collection problem." They have the items already. Furthermore, although an ongoing conversation about preserving history no doubt exists, the real conversation may well be around current events—even if it is about how one can better understand current events by understanding historical events. Are there elements of America's engagement in Iraq and Afghanistan that remind veterans of the conflict in Korea? Might politics, a revised GI bill, and health care be more important conversations? Certainly these conversations may include history and be informed by artifacts (photos, letters, etc.), but history and artifacts are only in service to new knowledge. Rather than looking at these communities as walking repositories of documents and history, librarians must see them as learners with much to offer other learners of different generations.

So if not a documentcentric approach, what should the Free Library do? The Free Library of Philadelphia and WHYY, the public broadcasting station serving the Philadelphia market, jointly developed the Coming of Age concept. The program would build on a successful initiative that trains nonprofits and provides connections via the website ComingofAge.org. The Free Library and WHYY envisioned "civic space" where people age 50+ can explore their future and address the needs of their generation as well as of society. Using a mix of technology, content, and physical public library and public broadcasting spaces, the program would be developed as a national model to encourage targeted education, community development, and ongoing social engagement of a growing and powerful set of citizens.

The centerpiece of the project, if built, would be an advanced social network that would let active older Americans connect with each other based on geography, topics, and activities. Coming of Age would allow older Americans not only to connect but also to prioritize learning opportunities by including a platform for creating online courses in which experienced retirees can pass on their knowledge in the areas of health care, finance, community engagement, and so on. Although the social network site would contain a large stable of multimedia materials from WHYY, the focus of the "collection" would be production facilities that would be made available to Coming of Age users to create their own histories, educational materials, and interactive documentaries. The Free Library would then bring together a consortium of public libraries creating in-person and place-based services to amplify the online work of users. For example, older Americans would be encouraged to become mentors to disadvantaged youth. This mentoring would happen online and at public libraries that provide safe spaces for active older Americans to meet mentees or each other. Public libraries could also provide basic training for members needing technical support. It is in this rich collection of online and in-person conversations that the true knowledge of active older Americans would be captured and put to immediate use.

THE ROLE OF THE LIBRARIAN

In the preceding example, the library provided a place, an infrastructure, and some elements of a collection. So, where was the librarian? If the primary task in serving active older Americans is to get them talking, does that mean that librarians who are not themselves older are sidelined? Far from it. Remember the four types of facilitation that are part of the participatory librarianship concept: access, knowledge, environment, and motivation. In the Coming of Age example, librarians are needed for each type of facilitation. As Mates (2004) points out, "As those who work in public service will attest, listening, practicing good humor, and displaying patience go a long way in making people feel comfortable. Making older patrons feel comfortable in a learning environment is a good start to computer literacy."

Take access, for example. True, the physical library provides a meeting place and Internet connectivity, but it will be librarians who must help active older Americans find their place within Coming of Age. It will be librarians who are constantly combing the public conversations of project members to identify necessary ideas and artifacts that will enhance conversations. In terms of knowledge, librarians will serve as coaches to bring project members up to speed in technical skills, as well as understanding the necessary history of a given conversation. It is the respected voice, policies, and service orientation of librarians that will ensure that Coming of Age represents a safe place for new members as well as ensuring a general sense of civility throughout the system. Finally, librarians will be needed to identify the motivations of project members and recognize them accordingly. Librarians, for example, would spotlight the work of members and groups of members for public recognition.

Whether or not Coming of Age is ever implemented, the planning and thinking processes demonstrate where a focus on conversation rather than collections leads. The primary service is the social network, for example, not the multimedia resources. The focus is the conversation, not the stuff used in the conversation. To use a crude analogy, a documentcentric library sits with a shovel at one end of the conversation and a catcher's mitt at the other. At the start of a learning process, the library stands ready to shovel loads of documents and materials for someone to wade through. The knowledge seeker then engages in the learning process, and if the result of that process happens to be a document (a book, article, web page, etc.), the library has plenty of processes for finding, cataloging, and disseminating the outcome. The main message of participatory librarianship is that the library must be a part of each aspect of the learning process, and most of those aspects don't involve artifacts.

THE POWER OF CONVERSATIONS ACROSS GENERATIONS

Libraries are uniquely and well poised to both gather knowledge from active older Americans and facilitate cross-generational conversations. In public libraries, for example, services have long targeted both older Americans and youth. In academic libraries, the increased emphasis on programs for retirees in higher education provides the opportunity to cross generational boundaries more easily than in the past. School libraries can now take advantage of increased participation by grandparents in the lives of their students.

America is getting older, and institutions of all types are scrambling to react and realign. In libraries, this means not only new services but also a better understanding of how current services can focus more on the knowledge seeking of active older Americans and less on their reading habits. Today's older Americans are more active, more informed, and more technologically literate than their predecessors. They represent not only the past but the lessons and experience of the past that are so vital to our future. Libraries must play a pivotal role in both developing new knowledge in active older Americans and in transferring this knowledge to younger generations. They will do so by focusing on learning and conversation, not on materials and artifacts.

REFERENCES

CDC Centers for Disease Control and Prevention. 2007. *National vital statistics reports* 56, no. 9 (December 28). www.cdc.gov/nchs/data/nvsr/nvsr56/nvsr56_09.pdf.

Chaffin, A. J., and S. D. Harlow. 2005. Cognitive learning applied to older adult learners and technology. *Educational Gerontology* 31:301–29.

Himes, C. L. 2003. Which U.S. states are the "oldest"? Washington, DC: Population Reference Bureau. www.prb.org/Articles/2003/WhichUSStatesAretheOldest.aspx.

Mates, B. T. 2004. Seniors and computer technology. *Library Technology Reports* 40 (3): 32–40.

Pask, G. 1976. *Conversation theory: Applications in education and epistemology.* New York: Elsevier.

OLD DOGS, NEW TRICKS
The Myths and the Realities

Stephen Abram

12

This chapter will address the role of libraries in serving the large, emerging 55+ market niche of users. This group was one of the largest population cohorts in history (until the Millennials came along), and its members will continue to influence and change public institutions as they age. In this chapter I will focus on the technological impacts of an aging population as well as the opportunities for great library programs that have a positive impact on our communities and the world at large. I will also outline some of the design considerations for older adult users. Libraries have always played a role in making communities great and serving as a form of nonpartisan social glue. As older adults change society with their increased facility with technology and the Web, we should be encouraged to shatter some of the myths about older adults and technology, IM, Facebook, searching, communication, and so on. It's time for libraries to set priorities for the development of 55+-friendly programs and services, establishing not only a physical but also a virtual presence. This chapter offers some guidance and ideas for progress.

Jakob Nielsen, web usability guru at the Nielsen Norman Group, stated that his study showing a number of issues with the usability of many websites for older adults was predictable.

> Given that most websites are produced by young people who probably take it for granted that all Web users have perfect vision and motor control, we weren't surprised that the seniors had a tougher time with the tasks than the younger test participants. What did surprise us is what good sports the seniors were about it. They tended to see the positive parts in generally negative experiences. They enjoyed a good challenge. (Nielsen 2002)

Older adults are one of the fastest-growing demographics on the Web, a trend that is not likely to slow down given the dramatic increase in the human life span. This trend is particularly important to library strategists because it means that the diversity of users of our virtual initiatives is likely increasing much faster than our ability to create programs and services. Because the consumer market has extensively catered to the boomer population, we can expect boomers to be equally demanding and have high expectations of their community and public institutions. This will be an exciting challenge for libraries.

THE NEW OLDER ADULT LIBRARY USER

Changing demographics have delivered a very different older adult user. For the purposes of this chapter, I will use the Pew Internet and American Life data (Jones and Fox 2009), shown in table 12.1.

In January 2009, the Pew Internet and American Life Project released new data on the proportion of generations online (see figure 12.1) and their behaviors online (see tables 12.2, 12.3, and 12.4). The key tables and charts reproduced here show much about what we can expect in the future from 55+ users.

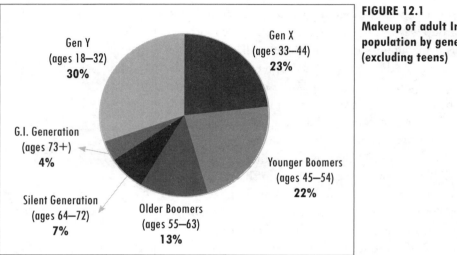

FIGURE 12.1
Makeup of adult Internet population by generation (excluding teens)

TABLE 12.1   Pew Internet and American Life data: Generations Explained

GENERATION NAME[a]	BIRTH YEARS, AGES IN 2009	PERCENTAGE OF TOTAL ADULT POPULATION[b]	PERCENTAGE OF INTERNET-USING POPULATION[c]
Gen Y (Millennials)	Born 1977–1990, ages 18–32	26%	30%
Gen X	Born 1965–1976, ages 33–44	20%	23%
Younger Boomers	Born 1955–1964, ages 45–54	20%	22%
Older Boomers	Born 1946–1954, ages 55–63	13%	13%
Silent Generation	Born 1937–1945, ages 64–72	9%	7%
G.I. Generation	Born before 1936, age 73+	9%	4%

Source: Pew Internet and American Life Project December 2008 survey

a All generation labels used in this report, with the exception of "Younger" and "Older" Boomers, are the names conventionalized by William Strauss and Neil Howe in *Generations: The History of America's Future, 1584 to 2069* (1991). As for "Younger Boomers" and "Older Boomers," research suggests that the two decades of baby boomers are different enough to merit being placed into distinct generational groups.

b *n* = 2,253 total adults; margin of error ±2%

c *n* = 1,650 total Internet users; margin of error ±3%

TABLE 12.2   Differences in Online Behavior by Age

	ONLINE TEENS (12–17)	GEN Y (18–32)	GEN X (33–44)	YOUNGER BOOMERS (45–54)	OLDER BOOMERS (55–63)	SILENT GENERATION (64–72)	G.I. GENERATION (73+)	ALL ONLINE ADULTS
Go online	93%	87%	82%	79%	70%	56%	31%	74%
Teens and Gen Yers are more likely to engage in the following activities compared with older users:								
Play games online	78	50	38	26	28	25	18	35
Watch videos online	57	72	57	49	30	24	14	52
Get information about a job	30~	64	55	43	36	11	10	47
Send instant messages	68	59	38	28	23	25	18	38
Use social networking sites (SNS)	65	67	36	20	9	11	4	35
Download music	59	58	46	22	21	16	5	37
Create SNS profile	55	60	29	16	9	5	4	29
Read blogs	49	43	34	27	25	23	15	32
Create a blog	28	20	10	6	7	6	6	11
Visit a virtual world	10	2	3	1	1	1	0	2
Activities where Gen X users or older generations dominate:								
Get health information	28	68	82	74	81	70	67	75
Buy something online	38	71	80	68	72	56	47	71
Bank online	*	57	65	53	49	45	24	55
Visit governmentt sites	*	55	64	62	63	60	31	59
Get religious information	26~	31	38	42	30	30	26	35
And for some activities, the youngest and oldest cohorts may differ, but there is less variation overall:								
Use e-mail	73	94	93	90	90	91	79	91
Use search engines	*	90	93	90	89	85	70	89
Research products	*	84	84	82	79	73	60	81
Get news	63	74	76	70	69	56	37	70
Make travel reservations	*	65	70	69	66	69	65	68
Research for job	*	51	59	57	48	33	9	51
Rate a person or product	*	37	35	29	30	25	16	32
Download videos	31~	38	31	21	16	13	13	27
Participate in an online auction	*	26	31	27	26	16	6	26
Download podcasts	19	25	21	19	12	10	10	19

Source: Based on Pew Internet and American Life Project surveys. Margins of error vary by subgroup; see methodology.

TABLE 12.3   Online Pursuits by Generation

RANK	GEN Y	GEN X	YOUNGER BOOMERS	OLDER BOOMERS	SILENT GENERATION	G.I. GENERATION
1	E-mail	E-mail	E-mail	E-mail	E-mail	E-mail
2	Search	Search	Search	Search	Search	Search
3	Research product	Research product	Research product	Get health information	Research product	Get health information
4	Get news	Get health information	Get health information	Research product	Get health information	Make travel reservations
5	Watch video	Buy something	Get news	Buy something	Make travel reservations	Research product
6	Buy something	Get news	Make travel reservations	Get news	Visit government site	Buy something
7	Get health information	Make travel reservations	Buy something	Make travel reservations	Buy something	Get news
8	Visit SNS*	Bank	Visit government site	Visit government site	Get news	Visit government site
9	Make travel reservations	Visit government site	Research for job	Bank	Bank	Get religious information
10	Get job information	Research for job	Bank	Research for job	Research for job	Bank
11	Create SNS profile	Watch video	Watch video	Get job information	Get religious information	IM
12	IM*	Get job information	Get job information	Watch video	Rate product	Play games
13	Download music	Download music	Get religious information	Rate product	Play games	Rate product
14	Bank	IM	Rate product	Get religious information	IM	Read blog
15	Visit government site	Get religious information	IM	Play games	Watch video	Watch video
16	Research for job	Play games	Auction	Auction	Read blog	Download video
17	Play games	Visit SNS	Read blog	Read blog	Auction	Get job information
18	Read blog	Rate product	Play games	IM	Download music	Podcast
19	Download video	Read blog	Download music	Download music	Download video	Research for job
20	Rate product	Download video	Download video	Download video	Get job information	Auction
21	Get religious information	Auction	Visit SNS	Podcast	Visit SNS	Create blog
22	Auction	Create SNS profile	Podcast	Visit SNS	Podcast	Download music
23	Podcast	Podcast	Create SNS profile	Create SNS profile	Create blog	Visit SNS
24	Create blog	Create blog	Create blog	Create blog	Create SNS profile	Create SNS profile
25	Visit virtual world	Visit virtual world	Visit virtual world	Visit virtual world	Visit virtual world	Visit virtual world

* SNS = social networking site; IM = instant message

Key: Percentage of Internet users in each generation who engage in this online activity

90–100%
80–89%
70–79%
60–69%
50–59%
40–49%
30–39%
20–29%
10–19%
0–9%

Above this line, over 50% of Internet users in the given generation engage in this online activity.

TABLE 12.4   Overall Online Pursuits

RANK	TEENS	GEN Y	GEN X	YOUNGER BOOMERS	OLDER BOOMERS	SILENT GENERATION	G.I. GENERATION
1	Play games	E-mail	E-mail	E-mail	E-mail	E-mail	E-mail
2	E-mail	Search	Search	Search	Search	Search	Search
3	Instant message (IM)	Research product	Research product	Research product	Get health information	Research product	Get health information
4	Visit social networking site (SNS)	Get news	Get health information	Get health information	Research product	Get health information	Make travel reservations
5	Get news	Watch video	Buy something	Get news	Buy something	Make travel reservations	Research product
6	Download music	Buy something	Get news	Make travel reservations	Get news	Visit government site	Buy something
7	Watch video	Get health information	Make travel reservations	Buy something	Make travel reservations	Buy something	Get news
8	Create SNS profile	Visit SNS	Bank	Visit government site	Visit government site	Get news	Visit government site
9	Read blog	Make travel reservations	Visit government site	Research for job	Bank	Bank	Get religious information
10	Buy something	Get job information	Research for job	Bank	Research for job	Research for job	Bank
11	Download video	Create SNS profile	Watch video	Watch video	Get job information	Get religious information	IM
12	Get job information	IM	Get job information	Get job information	Watch video	Rate product	Play games
13	Create blog	Download music	Download music	Get religious information	Rate product	Play games	Rate product
14	Get health information	Bank	IM	Rate product	Get religious information	IM	Read blog
15	Get religious information	Visit government site	Get religious information	IM	Play games	Watch video	Watch video
16	Podcast	Research for job	Play games	Auction	Auction	Read blog	Download video
17	Visit virtual world	Play games	Visit SNS	Read blog	Read blog	Auction	Get job information
18		Read blog	Rate product	Play games	IM	Download music	Podcast
19		Download video	Read blog	Download music	Download music	Download video	Research for job
20		Rate product	Download video	Download video	Download video	Get job information	Auction
21		Get religious information	Auction	Visit SNS	Podcast	Visit SNS	Create blog
22		Auction	Create SNS profile	Podcast	Visit SNS	Podcast	Download music
23		Podcast	Podcast	Create SNS profile	Create SNS profile	Create blog	Visit SNS
24		Create blog	Create blog	Create blog	Create blog	Create SNS profile	Create SNS profile
25		Visit virtual world	Visit virtual world	Visit virtual world	Visit virtual world	Visit virtual world	Visit virtual world

Types of activities:
Information seeking and research
E-commerce and online shopping
Entertainment
Communication and social media

At this point, 45 percent of 70–75-year-olds are online (see figure 12.2). Despite the disproportionate percentage of young people online, we'd be wise to recall that the younger cohort will move through the demographic curve, and we can expect future 55+ patrons to be significantly more online. Virtually all age cohorts were increasing their online access between 2005 and 2008.

Although home Internet access is increasing quickly in all age cohorts, we know that virtually all Americans have access to broadband Internet at home, work, school, or the local library (see figure 12.3). This is a transformational platform. The library plays a key role in bridging the various groups' access to technology (including printers, scanners, searching help, etc.) as well as integrating access to both hard-copy and electronic information along with training and support. Over the coming years the number of devices accessing the Internet will increase dramatically, including phones, cars, radios, games, and music players. This jump in access creates a very different world where ubiquitous connectivity and a variety of formats, going beyond text into moving images and sound, greatly change the expectations of users about what comprises a positive information experience. This change is much bigger than the one created by television in the middle of the last century, and that change was transformational, too.

SPECIAL NEEDS OF 55+ LIBRARY USERS

So there you have it. These 55+ users are a significant proportion of library users and deserve to be treated as a savvy market, regardless of the presence of a minority of e-challenged users. In many respects we have the services we need for the non-web-literate. We call those traditional services, and they don't need as much strategic attention at this point. What does need strategic attention is the emerging cohort of 55+ users who are quite different from the traditional seniors in libraries. There are specific differences in their needs and interests. They have been using computers as a cohort for decades, and many participated and continue to participate in the development of these tools and innovations.

Two key areas require special focus. First is the physical changes that occur naturally as we age. Indeed, some devices and website designs are not optimized for an older market. This lack of usability is not good if one is targeting that market! Barring the discovery of the Fountain of Youth, the issue of usability must be addressed. Second, our interests change as we mature (or at least get older!). The interest of older adults in story hours, for example, is likely to be for their grandchildren rather than their children. We also know that increased population mobility means families are spread far and wide—all over the United States and the world—and that many in war zones have a strong Web connectivity to home. Also, the long-term trend of family disruption through divorce and blended families means many older adults are dealing with friend and family relationships that are quite complex. This complexity means that electronic communication will increase in importance. In addition, topics of less personal interest to younger users, like genealogy, personal investing, pensions, retirement, and some personal health issues, are significantly more interesting for older users.

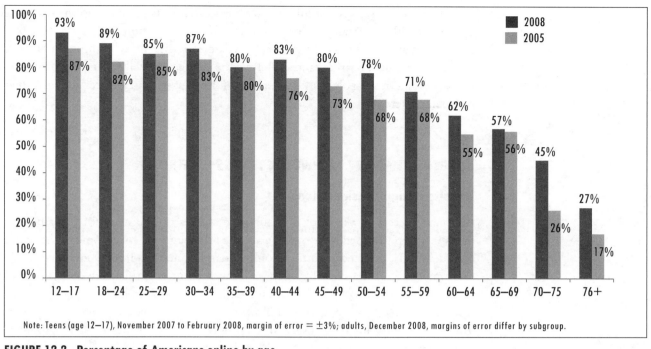

FIGURE 12.2   Percentage of Americans online by age

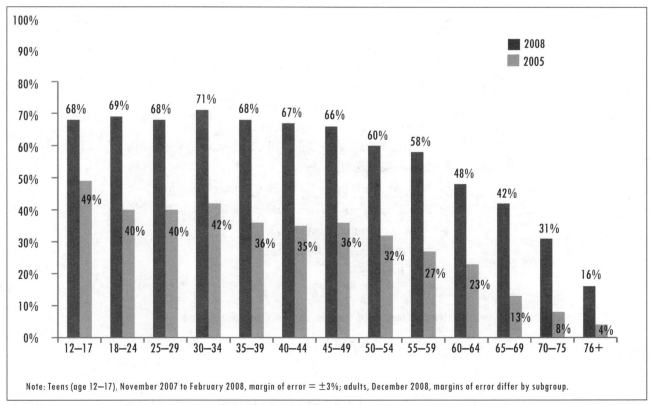

FIGURE 12.3   Percentage of all Americans with broadband at home by age

The next two sections of this chapter focus on these two issues and the changing dynamic of library strategies for 55+ users. The next section will explore adaptations necessary to address the physical needs of 55+ users, including such areas as eyesight, flexibility, hearing, and mobility. The last section will discuss opportunities for addressing this sizable market's demands for programs and services aimed at their particular interests.

ADAPTING LIBRARY TECHNOLOGY TO 55+ PATRONS

Website Design Considerations

Although there is a wealth of literature and studies on the needs of older participants in computer-mediated experiences, the following lists cover some of the major considerations. Selected reports, recommendations, and studies are included in the recommended readings for this chapter. However, much of this work owes a debt of gratitude to the work of Jakob Nielsen and the Nielsen Norman Group.

General research supports the following website design choices to increase comfort and usability for older users. Interestingly these guidelines generally apply to younger users as well, although for different reasons. Teens and young adults tend to be outliers on issues of color, smaller font size, and variety.

- ✦ Use sans serif typefaces such as Arial and Helvetica. Avoid condensed or narrow fonts and serif or novelty typefaces.
- ✦ Use 12- or 14-point font size for body text.
- ✦ Ensure that text is not frozen and can be adjusted by the user. (Many older users are quite comfortable setting the defaults in their browsers to enlarged text.)
- ✦ Use medium weight or boldface type.
- ✦ Don't use all caps except in headlines.
- ✦ Use underlining for links only, and ensure followed links change color.
- ✦ Double-space all body text.
- ✦ Use left justification for body text for older adults.
- ✦ Avoid using yellow, blue, and green in proximity.
- ✦ Avoid patterned backgrounds.
- ✦ Avoid unnecessary animation.
- ✦ Less is more.

Website Content and Organization Considerations

- ✦ Write with a positive tone and strive for simplicity and familiarity.
- ✦ Use the active voice and simple plain language, avoiding jargon. Remember that the older generational cohort is quite diverse with respect to speaking English as a new language.
- ✦ Use standard formats, and strive for consistency.

- Break up long text pieces into smaller chunks, especially text that will be read on-screen.
- Do not display text so that it runs landscape style on the full monitor.
- Ensure that images are relevant to the content.
- Use icons and symbols consistently.
- Strive for straightforward organization of the website.
- Ensure all icons have associated text and tell the story they are meant to tell.
- Use pull-down menus sparingly.
- Avoid flash animations.
- Avoid unnecessary application downloads.

Website Usability and Training Considerations

- Ensure that help by telephone and electronic means is easily identifiable and available. Help should be available at every point and not require backtracking to a home page.
- Allow for feedback. Respond to feedback in a timely manner.
- Reduce barriers to entry, such as difficult bar code sign-in pages.
- Allow for testing of adaptive technologies for users with vision, hearing, fine motor skill, and mobility issues.
- The Nielsen Norman Group website (www.nngroup.com) design rules are a good place to start with respect to design consistency.

Usability testing and some research show that the 55+ user has core needs similar to those of all users but that there are some life stage differences that are worthy of focus and consideration.

INFORMATION NEEDS AND THE 55+ USER

The "Generations Online in 2009" report from the Pew Internet and American Life Project (Jones and Fox 2009) discovered that more than 50 percent of 55+ web users used the Web to

1. E-mail
2. Search
3. Get health information
4. Research products
5. Buy something
6. Get news
7. Make travel reservations
8. Visit government sites

Significant numbers of 55+ web-accessing adults also used the Web to

1. Bank
2. Do research for a job
3. Get job information
4. Watch a video
5. Play games
6. Rate products

7. Participate in auctions

8. Get religious information

9. Read blogs

10. IM

A small but significant number of 55+ web users created social networking site profiles, blogged, podcasted, or downloaded music. Don't ignore these activities, because they will grow as the younger demographic cohort ages and continues its current Internet behaviors. Indeed the numbers are likely similar to those of many hobbies, such as philately, numismatics, genealogy, or gardening, which most libraries have no trouble supporting.

Topics that float to the top as key subjects of interest in the 55+ cohort include health, finance, travel, sports, religion, genealogy, politics and advocacy, news (local, national, homeland, and foreign), hobbies, and retirement. Each individual user in this group has quite personal and specific goals. Unlike young users who may be exploring a wide range of issues within these topical areas for educational or personal reasons, older users are often specifically interested in their own or a loved one's health condition, their own financial situation, their own family's history, and the news from their homeland or in their other language. They are usually not trying to cast about widely for general information but are seeking information that matches their specific interests and often their own points of view. The challenge for librarians is to assist and train this group in broad searching skills rather than finely tuned "finding" skills. Added to this is an increasing awareness of the need for safety, confidentiality, and privacy skills.

To address the program needs of 55+ users, we need to understand the specific activities they are undertaking and determine how library staff and programs might assist and improve the experience. Core end-user considerations involved in these types of web pursuits include the following:

✦ fact finding and searching

✦ comparing and contrasting

✦ retrieving information

✦ buying an item (retail, web only, or auction)

✦ conducting banking, insurance, investment, and financial transactions

✦ communicating (e-mail)

✦ learning

✦ managing privacy and money

Each of these pursuits comes with its own set of issues and challenges. Because 55+ users did not grow up with an education system that taught critical information literacy skills in an Internet environment, their skills can be a hodgepodge of competencies, likely learned on the fly at work or play. These skills also cover the gamut in this cohort from expert to naive. Libraries can play a key role in this environment. With respect to search and fact-finding activities, for example, older adults need to develop critical information evaluation skills. These skills are especially important for key subjects like health, politics, and travel. Because many people in the 55+ cohort buy things online using credit cards and sharing personal information, libraries can teach safety measures for online purchases, including the identification and reporting of scams. Building stronger skills for navigating online financial environments (banking, pensions, insurance, stocks, etc.) is also a unique opportunity for libraries.

Although e-mail is now routine for almost all web cohorts of 55+ users, a good deal of training is required for instant messaging and communicating among the generations as well as for appropriate social networking behaviors and the sharing of pictures, videos, and recordings. Many older adults are also very involved in e-learning. They may have been laid off from companies affected by changes in the economy and find their core skills no longer in high demand. They choose to take courses on the Web or local courses that include an online learning or research component. You can see the high number of 55+ users who spend time job seeking online in the Pew data (Jones and Fox 2009). Some retire or semi-retire and start to study topics that may or may not be related to their work life. E-learning allows them to explore interests that may have been postponed for many years. A few even turn these avocations into paying work. And some are just lifelong learners. It is interesting how many discover, or rediscover, the library as their partner in these pursuits. Teaching meta-learning skills and how to use the suites of skills required to adapt to new modes of learning in an e-learning environment is another opportunity for libraries. Of course, many of these skills involve just the sorts of applications in which libraries are becoming expert: wikis, collaboration environments, blogs, and other Web 2.0 applications.

This is the background of the 55+ library user at the start of the twenty-first century. As a group they are neither poor nor rich, strong nor feeble, healthy nor unhealthy, or anything else that pigeonholes them into some narrow stereotype that limits their skills, abilities, and opportunities. By most measures this is a cohort that is very supportive of libraries, so engaging and delighting them has positive benefits on many levels.

The last section of this chapter focuses on various programs for libraries to consider implementing for the emerging 55+ cohort of users. Integrating the new technological context of Web 2.0 into these ideas is part of the plan. It's not necessary for the technology to lead or be obvious, but it does help to make these tactics leap off the page.

LEARNING, COMMUNITY, AND PROGRAMS FOR THE 55+ USER

The emerging challenge is to break the mold that largely considers programs to have a date, place, and time. Although these can be great programs and many are listed here, all types of programming need to be considered. Other options include asynchronous programming, such as e-learning and web-based programs, as well as asymmetrical programming (programming that does not have to follow a regular schedule, such as drop-in events). The web technologies that are largely collected under the rubric of Web 2.0 or Library 2.0 offer many opportunities for innovation. In the following program suggestions, I mention a number of useful topics, but it is the format that I'd like you to consider as the program.

The Local Library Gardening Club Wiki

Build a wiki for your local gardeners. Involve local gardening clubs as partners. You could even partner with local nurseries and greenhouses. You have the basics already: you collect books that align with gardening in your climate, and you answer questions. With a wiki, people can share tips, trade shoots and plants, review books (and plants) for your climate zone, and meet up at the library (inside or in the parking lot/garden). Consider putting the gardening collection on a cart and joining the sidewalk sales during planting season or move it right into the Garden Center. Build a collaborative blog, with photos of successful gardens and plants. Make the library plantings a community garden initiative. This is the library at its best—as social glue.

Podcasting for Adults: Sharing Community Stories

Do your local folks have stories? Yes, they do. Scratch anyone and she or he has stories and memories of your town. Collecting local history has gotten so easy. Set up podcasting days to record your folks' stories. Try theme days—the state fair; memories of WWII, Korea, the Great Depression, or the Sixties. Collect these stories, add them to your blog and iTunes, and you've got a library radio station broadcasting interesting community memories. I'll bet you find a few stars of the spoken word.

Teens and Seniors Partnerships—The Flickr Event

Just about everyone has a digital camera (or can borrow one). Are you looking for ways to bridge the gap between the teens in your community and older folks? It's easy. Send the teens out on a mission. Ask them to take pictures of important places or events about town. Again, you can choose a theme—historic buildings, local fairs, school events, elections—then ask them to load the photos on Flickr (teach them CC [Creative Commons] licensing, too). Next, have a group of interested adults organize the photos using tags and labels and blog them into a story. Ultimately, you'll end up having the best visual tourist site in town! And you'll have bridged the generation gap, too.

Building Our Local History Vault—Scanning and Flickr Again

Have you heard about library scanning parties? It's a safe bet that the 55+ user has boxes of old photos (not hard drives' full). Set aside a Saturday or Sunday morning. Connect an easy scanner to a PC and ask folks to come in and share their photos. Set a limit (for example, twelve photos per family), and choose a theme: The Fifties: The World in Black and White, Christmas (or any celebration) through the Years, Fun on the Farm (or in the City), or My Homeland/Roots. Folks get excited about searching their photos and selecting the best to share with the community. Again, the social glue strengthens, and people share their experiences. It all goes into an image database that grows, and people learn tagging skills, blogging the photos, and creating albums and online exhibits. It's a wild ride that can grow the library's presence and impact on communities and connect to the 55+ patron.

Telling Kids' Stories—Podcasting Made Easy

Do your users have a favorite children's story? Has someone made one up? Is there a classic story (that is to say, out of copyright) that users love? Ask them to come to the library and record the classic or original stories that the children they care about loved. It's simple, and the stories will be archived in the library for every local child to hear. There's storytelling talent out there to be captured. You can even include stories in heritage languages. You'll likely be pleasantly surprised at the voice talents of your users and the passion they put into a project like this. A side benefit is that this program inexpensively adds new resources to the library collection for prereaders, adds bedtime stories to your collection for use at home, and helps visually impaired kids. It can all start when you engage your 55+ neighbors.

The New News: Finding the News That You Care About Online

Newspapers, sadly, are closing or shrinking quite quickly. Most urban areas are limited to one local daily. Readers in the 55+ age range grew up in an era when news came on paper, TV, or radio. Now people have access to an enormous number of news sources, including online magazines and radio and TV available on the Web or through their local library's resources. Times have changed. Is everyone ready to handle the deluge? This is where the library steps in. Teaching searching, RSS, aggregator, and quality evaluation and discovery skills is a big opportunity. One of the top online papers in the United States is published in the United Kingdom. People are casting their nets widely to be better informed and to address the decline of the print media. The 55+ patron is a key target market for this training. The magic is in addressing these users' specific goals, not just generic news. Focus on their top topics like health, finance, and hobbies.

[Insert Major Ethnic or Language Group Here] and the Web

You know the census results for your area. What are the top ethnic and language groups in your catchment areas and communities? Where are people's homelands? What are the local clubs and associations that are based on ethnicity? Often, in the 55+ cohort, this localization can be a strength or a weakness. You may have a built-in social group, or you may have a prescription for isolation and loneliness. These groups may also be less connected to the Internet than other groups are. Here's where libraries can play a big role. Teach folks how to reconnect with the news in their first language or from their homelands where friends and relatives may still reside. Teaching them how to use Skype and free long distance can have obvious benefits. You don't really need to know their language to be successful in this strategy—they're the experts here. Dive in and make a difference. Again it's not about the technology but the engagement with users to meet their social and information needs.

Blogging for the Next Generation from the Big One

Setting up the library as a place for adults to blog is an interesting concept. Can your library identify community leaders (or create a place for community leadership to emerge)? Do you have someone like Nancy Pearl, the famous librarian, author, and NPR book reviewer, in your community? Who are your chief book lovers? Can they blog for you? Can they comment on what they read and make recommendations? I suspect the answer is yes. Is your library open *enough* to your communities?

Hidden Dollars—Getting the Most Out of Auction Sites

We know that older adults often have too much stuff. Yet they buy more and sell quite a bit online. Some of the best-selling Dummies series books are the ones about eBay and online auctions. We also know that this process is fraught with risk unless it is well understood. Many libraries are full of books and electronic resources that assist users in identifying antiques and collectibles and in valuing items. Libraries could do very well in offering training and advice in handling these new economic opportunities. In fiscally difficult times, the library can step up to assist with these online yard sales on steroids.

Modern Writing Skills: Getting Published

On the popular 43 Things website (www.43things.com), one of the most common things that people want to do is write—a book, poetry, short stories, a play. Many people find that with their children grown or with retirement setting in, they now have enough time to fulfill this dream. Of course, they don't know where to start, where to publish, where to get advice, and so on. What a wonderful opportunity for libraries. We already have the resources to help folks. Now, can we develop programs, using the wonderful 2.0 tools now available, to connect latent writers to other writers, to support groups, to training at the library and beyond? Can we provide a place for them to publish their first creations? It can start with a blog or a short-story writing contest or a poetry jam. It can start with a coffeehouse atmosphere or in a classroom setting.

Driving to Florida (or Wherever) with Kids

Imagine (or remember) driving from New York to Florida with three kids in the backseat. What do you need to know to make this ride bearable or even pleasant? Think of a program that recommends books for the ride to each kid. Think of a program that shares games and tricks for making the ride great. Think of travel planning for kids and finding sites of interest along the way. Think of a program that shares what kids are interested in today—have they grown past J. K. Rowling to Stephenie Meyer? Is it EverQuest, Wii, or WoW? Is "sick" in or out? "What's hot and what's not" training for the 55+ set. I'll bet Young Adult librarians can program for older folks, too.

Online Financial Planning for the 55+ Adult

The 55+ user is more focused than any other demographic group on financial issues: retirement, part-time work, wills and estates, health insurance, and more. Libraries have the collections and resources to support these topics and often provide programming to assist this group. Through partnerships and effective design of web-based information resources, the library can make a difference.

Internet Safety for Older Adults

Kids aren't the only ones who need awareness and competency training in safe Internet use. The solution isn't in blocking sites but in developing individual and community competencies about personal information management, privacy, scams, phishing, viruses, and more, not only on general websites but also on online dating sites (one in eight Americans married in 2008 met online first), information sites, and health sites. We know from Pew research that the 55+ user visits financial management sites for online banking and investing and purchases items online at auction sites like eBay or on retail sites. We must build twenty-first-century skills in our communities, and libraries are best positioned to do this. Libraries that position themselves as sources of good advice can only delight their communities and create greater local success.

Great Grandparenting from a Distance: E-mail, Instant Messaging, Blogging, and More

Being a grandparent in today's world can be difficult. Families are spread out across the nation and around the world. Thousands of people are overseas fighting wars, and with most of these folks being Millennials and having quite facile skills with the new technologies, we have a communication technology gap that could disrupt families and our communities. Libraries can step in by offering training on and access to these services, which are mostly freely available. When libraries target 55+ users with embarrassment-free training in advanced e-mail, instant messaging, blogging, Skype, YouTube/TroopTube, and more, they connect patrons and their families in marvelous ways. Knowing the basics as well as more advanced skills, such as attaching photos, MP3 conversations, and so on, can create a world of difference for families separated by hundreds or thousands of miles.

Saving Money Online

As I write this chapter, the world is immersed in a difficult recession. Libraries do well in difficult times—we're often free and deliver good value! Use increases. Can we offer other money-saving tips to our patrons? Sure. How about a series of sessions on saving money with the Web? Individual sessions on saving money with research, Skype, coupons, tax preparation, and more can all be popular.

Wii Play, Too—Gaming for Adults

One of the surprises for me in the Pew Generations Online study was the high placement of gaming by 55+ Internet users. I think different games are involved, although there is probably some overlap. It seems that Wii, for example, is a gaming system that spans the generations. On the other hand, I'll wager that bridge, euchre, Jeopardy, Scrabble, crosswords, and so on trend to older populations in popularity. I hear that research shows that gaming activity helps in keeping brains and motor skills nimble and can potentially stave off Alzheimer's! Either way, electronic games are a far more social activity than usually thought, and, according to Scott Nicholson at Syracuse University, the vast majority of libraries offer gaming activities. It's time to think strategically about the demographic niches beyond teens when planning gaming programs.

"Borrow a Senior" with Your Library Card

A few libraries around the world offer the ability to borrow people—yes, people. For teachers, schools, recreation centers, and other cultural institutions, this is a great way to find free speakers and programs. People have life experiences and stories. How about folks talking about their collections, hobbies, travels, homelands, jobs? Another popular group might be veterans. Libraries can catalog people just as well as they catalog other resources!

Healthy Living: Health Information Online for the 55+ Adult

Health information is a top search request of the 55+ adult. And the Web is full of high-quality medical information along with loads of garbage. Finding the good information and advice and identifying what can be trusted are important skills for everyone. Libraries have access to quality print resources as well as the skills to teach how to access appropriate health information on the Web. We must also consider the proper alignment of health information with the medical literacy of each end user. Some patrons can be quite expert about their own condition while others are newbies just starting out.

Twenty-three Things for the 55+ Adult

Over the past two years, the 23 Things—Learning 2.0 movement worldwide has made a huge impact on libraries and their ability to deal with new technologies. Many libraries have extended this free, self-directed Web 2.0 skills training program to their communities as well. Learning about how to learn online, blogging, digital photos, RSS and newsreaders, wikis, portals, online applications like Google Docs, podcasts, streaming media, and digital audio in a group or community is very powerful. Many older adults find the 23 Things program very energizing and empowering as they learn to learn again and find that there are no barriers to achieving success in the web-oriented world.

Genealogy Online

Libraries have been riding the genealogy juggernaut for years. This is a top hobby of the 55+ cohort, and libraries have the skills to empower people to succeed even more at this family-oriented hobby. Because so much information is online, there are new skills and sites to learn every day. A library blog and online training course can make a huge impact. In addition, many libraries have photographed and indexed local cemeteries to attract ancestry tourism groups to their area.

Travel Tips Online: Planning Your Next Trip

Travel is different for the 55+ user. As a group, they have less demand for hostels and campsites and a greater chance of traveling long distances. Most travel is now booked online, and identifying hotels, destinations, side trips, and the like is not only an engaging process but also one that is filled with potential for fraud. Anticipation is half the trip! Training in finding the most exciting and useful sites online as well as sharing trips with neighbors represent opportunities for libraries.

Getting the Most Out of Your Mobile Phone: Introductory and Advanced

Virtually everyone has a mobile phone today. That doesn't necessarily mean that everyone is using their phone to its full potential. Indeed, many folks in the 55+ generations had VCRs and couldn't program them. The emergence of G3 smart phones has produced an even greater demand for training to use all the features on a cell phone. With the ability to access web and library services via the phone, it's in the best interests of libraries to provide help and advice.

YouTube: Tell Your Story

Has anyone missed the YouTube revolution? Just as we are experimenting with podcasts and blog postings for users to share stories and experiences with others, we can do the same thing with YouTube and other streaming media. Set up events to film older adults. People psychically connect to institutions that care about them and their opinions and needs. It's the library as theater!

Book Reviewing Skills

Libraries are about books for sure. And the world of books has changed immeasurably since Amazon.com arrived on the scene. A large part of Amazon's success goes beyond its vast inventory of new and used books to its capability for users to share their opinions with a community of readers. Can we bring this excitement into the library on an even greater scale? Initiatives such as LibraryThing for Libraries and BiblioCommons allow library cardholders to comment on and review books they have read. Some libraries have book review blogs that are shared by librarians and end users. Others use APIs (application programming interfaces) to link to information on the websites of Amazon.com, Borders, Barnes and Noble, and so forth. Are libraries prepared to encourage and train end users to share their opinions about books and reading on our blogs and websites and OPACs as well as the retail sites do? I think we are.

Website Links for (Older) Adults

Many libraries have web pages on their sites for "seniors." As we have seen throughout this chapter and this book, seniors are not a homogeneous population, and they have as much in common with the general web user population as they have differences. They do have special needs, but these might be better promoted through topical and interest-based pages. One way to target specialized messages is to use the birth date in the patron record. Lists of links that have not been developed to address the specific interests of this population are not as successful as they could be.

Social Networking for 55+ Users

Users in the 55+ age range are significantly less likely, at this point, to have a social networking profile than are younger demographic cohorts. Older Americans are more likely to suffer from shrinking social networks as they age. They may also desire to be connected to younger family members. Teaching the facts about social networking and its potential for connecting to friends and family can reap big benefits. It also allows people to make informed decisions about whether to participate. Where there is interest there is an opportunity for libraries to communicate, share, and play a role. Many libraries have Facebook and MySpace presences and are learning along with their users. Some have been successful in adding OPAC and reference services into their social sites.

CONCLUSION

So there you have it. If you follow the goals of good website design and ensure that your online presence is easy to learn, remember, and use, and if you combine that accessibility with real and virtual programs that are interesting and engaging, then you win. Your library wins, and your community wins. And the older adult is recognized as a viable and important market for customized library services.

RECOMMENDED READING (WITH THANKS TO K. DAVIS)

Bray, H. 2005. Adapting PCs to an aging population. *Boston Globe,* January 31. www
.boston.com/business/globe/articles/2005/01/31/adapting_pcs_to_an_aging_
population/.

Chadwick-Dias, A., D. Tedesco, and T. Tullis. 2004. Older adults and web usability: Is
web experience the same as web expertise? *Extended abstracts of the 2004 conference on
human factors and computing systems.* Conference on Human Factors in Computing
Systems, Vienna, Austria. New York: ACM Press, 1391–94.

Coyne, K. P., and J. Nielson. 2002. Usability for senior citizens. April 28. www.useit.com/
alertbox/20020428.html.

Davis, K. 2005. *Designing usable web sites for senior citizens.* University of Texas at Austin.
http://kristinmdavis.com/projects/usability_for_seniors.html.

Emerging tool helps to ensure accessibility and usability for the visually disabled. July 26,
2004. www.thematuremarket.com/SeniorStrategic/imprimer_texte.php?numtxt=
2665&idrb=5#.

Hanson, V. L. 2001. Web access for elderly citizens. *Workshop on Universal Accessibility of Ubiquitous Computing.* Proceedings of the 2001 EC/NSF workshop on universal accessibility of ubiquitous computing: Providing for the elderly. New York: ACM, 14–18. ACM Digital Library. http://portal.acm.org/citation.cfm?id=564526.564531.

Institute for Future Studies. 2007. Usability and ergonomics considerations on elearning of older adults. Austria, June 20. http://82.223.160.93/site/Output%202%20-%20 usability %20and%20ergonomics%20report.pdf.

Jones, S., and S. Fox. 2009. Generations online in 2009. Pew Internet and American Life Project. www.pewinternet.org/Reports/2009/Generations-Online-in-2009.aspx.

National Institute on Aging, National Library of Medicine, and National Institutes of Health. 2001. Making your web site senior friendly: A checklist. Washington, DC. www.nlm.nih.gov/pubs/staffpubs/od/ocpl/agingchecklist.html.

Nielsen Norman Group. Web usability for senior citizens: 46 design guidelines based on usability studies with people age 65 and older. www.nngroup.com/reports/seniors/.

Pew Internet and American Life Project. www.pewinternet.org.

Rosenfeld, L., and P. Morville. 1998. *Information architecture for the World Wide Web: Designing large-scale web sites.* Sebastopol, CA: O'Reilly.

Senior Learning: Adapting e-learning techniques for integrating senior citizens in the new digital world. 2008. Senior citizens e-learning needs report. Ulm University. September. http://82.223.160.93/site/Output%201%20-%20Senior%20Citizens %20elearning%20needs%20report.pdf.

Underhill, P. 1999. If you can read this you're too young. *Why we buy: The science of shopping.* New York: Simon and Schuster, 129–40.

Van Duyne, D. K., J. A. Landay, and J. I. Hong. 2003. The design of sites: Patterns, principles, and processes for drafting a customer centered web experience. Boston: Addison-Wesley.

REFERENCES

Jones, S., and S. Fox. 2009. Generations online in 2009. Pew Internet and American Life Project. www.pewinternet.org/Reports/2009/Generations-Online-in-2009 .aspx. See also Generations online: Charts. www.pewinternet.org/Presentations/ 2009/Generations-Online-in-2009.aspx.

Nielsen, J. 2002. Usability for senior citizens. www.useit.com/alertbox/seniors.html.

Strauss, W., and N. Howe. 1991. *Generations: The History of America's Future, 1584 to 2069.* New York: Morrow.

MUSINGS ON CHALLENGES FOR LIBRARIANS IN 2040

13

Pauline Rothstein

This chapter was prompted by a conversation with Diantha Schull about my reactions to the fast pace of technology growth in libraries and its implications for the future of libraries. As I thought about writing on the subject, I realized that I could not write about libraries for the future. I don't know that there will be libraries in the future. Even if I limit the future to thirty years, or the year 2040, I still can't imagine a library; however, I can imagine a *librarian* in the future. Institutions change over time. Historical and cultural circumstances change. Basic human needs do not change, although their attributes may.

In my initial search of documents on libraries for the future, I was struck by a publication from Idaho that reported the findings of a future-oriented task force dedicated to brainstorming about the reasons why digital natives will want to use libraries in the year 2020 (*Idaho's Library Future* 2006). In their imagining of the future, the task force participants focused on the needs of people, not the number of square feet in the library building. Figure 13.1, taken from the Idaho report, informs my speculation on the purpose of being a librarian in the year 2040. As a native New Yorker, I find it hard to admit that the best document I found on identifying human needs for libraries is from Idaho . . . but it is!

Just as the Idaho report informs my view of the future for librarians, the sage Ranganathan's laws provide me with another approach to librarianship. S. R. Ranganathan, the father of library science, promulgated the following Five Laws of Library Science.

1. Books are for use.
2. Every person his or her book.
3. Every book, its reader.
4. Save the time of the reader.
5. A library is a growing organism. (Ranganathan 1931)

How would Ranganathan write these laws for the twenty-first century?

1. Books, audiobooks, DVDs, e-content, chips, implants . . . are for use.
2. Every person his or her book, e-content, chip, implant . . .
3. Every book (e-content . . .) its reader (listener, attender, player, . . .).

These first three laws will change as time passes. The fourth will always be the librarian's purpose. The fifth applies to the library as it exists today and as it may

The Library is a place where I can
Invent
Study
Read for pleasure
Meet
Dream
Have coffee
See neighbors
Learn
Grow
Debate
Explore
Share ideas
Get ideas
Create ideas
Ask questions
Get answers
Talk to people with similar interests
Teach
Play
Develop my mind
Find knowledge
Be inspired
Touch the past . . . and the future

Source: *Idaho's Library Future* 2006, 5.

FIGURE 13.1   The Library Is a Place Where I Can

exist in the future. If there is no physical library, the fifth law applies to all the ways librarians can provide information. The Five Laws apply to older adults as well as to other demographic groups. The needs of older adults are not always addressed in the human community. For librarians they must be!

Bearing in mind these two very different frameworks for librarianship, I focused on three fundamental concerns that must also be central for librarianship in relation to older adults. These concerns include the increasing pace of technological innovation, the development of new insights into how the brain works, and the emerging science of happiness studies.

TECHNOLOGY

Stories about human needs fulfilled by new technology and the gadgets inspired by it make for interesting reading. The *New York Times* recognized this when, in 1998, it published the first Circuits section for the paper. The purpose of the section was to expand coverage of the kind of technology that "has already changed the lives of everyone. . . . [T]he new technologies built on the computer chip, and particularly how they affect everyday life, will be the subjects of the Circuits coverage." The first Circuits article had the headline "A Fetish for Order" and described the Palm Pilot personal organizer. The section also included articles on game theory, ergonomics, productivity, computing, crash triage, and the library: "CD-ROM encyclopedias offer a cornucopia of information, dressed up with multimedia pizzazz. But some may be nostalgic for the joys of a trip to the library" (*New York Times,* February 16, 1998).

By the year 2000 the *Times* hired David Pogue to do a regular personal tech column. As time went on, the paper moved the tech column to the business section on Thursday with an occasional special Circuits section. By March 2005 the *Times* integrated much of the technology writing into the daily paper with special coverage in the business section: "Circuits will no longer appear as a weekly stand-alone section beginning March 31. The majority of its features will be incorporated into a revamped Thursday Business Day. Other features from Circuits will be distributed throughout the newspaper" (*New York Times,* March 31, 2005). Currently, the *Times* also has a Technology/Media feature on Mondays.

Why this history of the *Times'* technology coverage? Because it is an obvious way to show how, in the past ten years, technology has progressed enough to take this subject from a special newspaper section intended for early adapters to an integral part of the paper and of life today. Many older adults use cell phones regularly, have the time and interest to download iTunes, take digital photographs, and communicate via e-mail with their grandchildren. Those retiring from full-time jobs and transitioning to part-time or volunteer work find that they have to learn to use new technology in new occupations. Even doing the laundry may require computerized cards linked to credit cards.

We do not know what technologies will exist in 2040. Nanotechnology? Green technologies? Librarians will keep up with the latest technologies—regular training programs will continue to be part of their lives. I am not worried about the ability of librarians to learn to use technology. I am concerned about the amount of time and effort they will spend to address the information needs of older adults. Will older adults want to read? I think so—whether on reading devices or electronic paper or in conventional books or via audio devices, the imaginative power of reading will provide as much pleasure to some people in 2040 as it does now. How will future librarians address what we used to call readers' advisory service? Will librarians read "books" and recommend them? Should they? If one reviews all the elements in figure 13.1, it is clear that the answer is yes.

THE HUMAN BRAIN

In the future, the successful librarian will be the professional who integrates the social, cultural, scientific, and technological developments in the 2040 world with a passion for and knowledge of the characteristics of older adults, however we define them in the future. These librarians will work toward engaging their constituents in productive and satisfying activities. To meet this challenge, librarians will have to keep up with discoveries about the human brain as it and its owner age. For it is the brain that houses all our human desires, skills, emotions, capacities, and abilities to invent, create, and communicate. Given the brain's importance, librarians will want to understand all the ways of thinking about the brain.

The conventional wisdom in America has been that our brain develops throughout childhood and adolescence and then stops growing when we reach adulthood. Furthermore, we've been told there is often a decline in "brain power" as people age. More recently, however, we have come to accept the new notion of *brain plasticity,* or continuous change (Cohen 2006).

This concept is not as new as it seems. The great Soviet neuropsychologist Alexander Luria (1907–1977) spent much of his life laying the foundation for what is now known as brain plasticity. Originally a psychologist, Luria trained as a physician. In Moscow, he treated brain trauma after World War II and headed a neuropsychology department and a laboratory. Here he researched the cognitive, cultural, and developmental interests that allowed him to pursue new notions about the brain, specifically, brain–behavior relationships. His competence in cognition (as a psychologist) and the brain (as a neurologist) informed his work. By the 1960s Luria had published sixteen books in English (Kazdin 2000).

Luria's system of flexible qualitative assessment of brain functions and his numerous studies showed that the brain is influenced by *culture* and *environment.* From this finding, he developed the concept of neuroplasticity—that is, the ability of the stimulated mind to change and adapt and even rewire itself (Goldberg 1990). This concept was greatly influenced by the work of Luria's colleague, Lev Vygotsky, who, with Luria, investigated thinking as a "culturally embedded activity" in studies of minority groups in Russia (Sheehy 2004).

Are Americans ready to accept the concept of brain plasticity? Yes. Now that there is a large cohort of older adults, we want to know what can be done to stave off the diseases of aging, especially those of the mind.

For those interested in a detailed description of how the brain works, how it changes as we age, and implications for working with older adults, Paul Nussbaum has produced an excellent introductory book, video, and DVD on the subject (www .paulnussbaum.com).

SharpBrains, a marketing and advisory group focused on cognitive health and brain fitness, makes keeping up with the latest practical and theoretical information on brain fitness both fun and intellectually challenging. *Hourglass,* a carnival of blogs on biogerontology hosted by SharpBrains, offers a monthly forum with up-to-date ideas on the biology of aging (http://ouroboros.wordpress.com/hourglass/). SharpBrains was cofounded in 2005 by Alvaro Fernandez, the host of *Hourglass,* and Elkhonon Goldberg, a neurologist and student of Alexander Luria's.

Learning about brain fitness strategies is important for librarians who work with older adults; however, it becomes even more useful when we look at how the brain operates in each of its hemispheres. For a long time it was thought that the right hemisphere ages more than the left over the same time. With the advent of the MRI (magnetic resonance imaging), neuroscientists could see the brain with significantly more clarity. New brain studies were conducted. What did they prove?

The right brain hemisphere ages at a faster rate than the left hemisphere (Goldberg 2005, 244).

What are the implications of this finding? The old "use it or lose it" adage is true when it comes to brainpower. We now know that new neurons in the brain can be "influenced by cognitive activities in a way not dissimilar from the manner in which muscle growth can be influenced by physical exercise" (Goldberg 2005, 247). Goldberg emphasizes the need to engage aging individuals in athletics and art to improve their brain's resistance to decay. His delightful discussion of the persistence of athletics and art from ancient times to today supports his recommendation for regular right brain cognitive exercise.

The work of Daniel Pink (2006), as described in his book *A Whole New Mind: Why Right-Brainers Will Rule the Future,* does more than describe the functions of the right and the left sides of the brain. Using a sociological approach, Pink contends that although left-brain functions have been rewarded in the recent past, the future belongs to the right-brained. Pink notes that our society has gone from one of scarcity to one of abundance. The computer has allowed outsourcing of much of the left-brain work. This evolution is responsible for the need for the human high-concept, high-tech aptitudes resident in the right brain. Pink puts it succinctly when he says that "now the new M.B.A is the M.F.A." (2006, 55). Even if we do not agree with this notion completely, Pink offers an exciting look at how attending to right-brain functions can lead to a new and more positive way of thinking about older adults and the aging process.

In the second part of his book, Pink offers a conceptual framework for implementing his ideas. Librarians can use the six dimensions of Pink's framework to generate innovative ways of bringing information and human needs together. The six dimensions are Design, Story, Symphony, Empathy, Play, and Meaning. Each dimension has specific illustrative activities for right-brain enrichment. The Symphony dimension, for example, refers to conceptual blending. Older adults who are freed from daily work in the formerly prominent left-brain professions are a perfect audience for this kind of right-brain activity.

HAPPINESS

Hope is definitely not the same thing as optimism. It is not the conviction that something will turn out well, but the certainty that something makes sense, regardless of how it turns out.

—Václav Havel, "Hope"

This quotation from Václav Havel's poem opens up a special way of thinking about the relationship between librarians and older adults. We know that a primary interest of adults in this group is in finding answers that are meaningful to them. They will accept answers that are not what they expect . . . they just want those answers to make sense. Librarians have the skill to bring people together with information that they need. While thinking about the happiness principles when they work with older adults, librarians can use their information-seeking skills to make people happy or to give them hope or to do both.

Fulfilling human needs is at the core of the librarian's job. Happiness is a universal human need. Measuring client happiness, as explained in recent happiness literature, is an important way to assess the success of any librarian–older adult interaction. A vivid description of what makes us happy is offered in a discussion of gaming. Gaming is popular because it fulfills multiple needs. A games researcher at the Institute for the Future has written an excellent analysis of game playing that explains its popularity (McGonigal 2009). This analysis has direct applicability to the structuring of activities for and with older adults. Jane McGonigal, resident designer of alternative reality games and research affiliate at the Institute for the Future, says that "mass collaboration in the virtual world can translate into helping communities in the real world probe the future and solve problems." The popularity of computer games is revealing in terms of the human needs they fulfill. Although the first home video game was invented only thirty-one years ago and therefore the average American gamer is 35 years old, studies show that as gamers grow up they don't stop. In fact, one in four gamers is over the age of 50. This development has implications for those who interact with older adults now and in the future (McGonigal 2009, 32).

What principles do game designers use to captivate the attention and take the time of so many people? They are principles based on "creating this kind of collective resource of mind share, heart share and energy" that encourages many people to spend upward of twenty hours a week playing games. McGonigal notes that the *science of happiness* is about understanding what the human brain is built for and what our emotional and social systems enable us to do so that we can optimize human experience. What is especially notable about game players is their diversity. Clearly, games make all kinds of people happy. They address the very human needs expressed by the words in figure 13.1.

The Four Principles of Happiness, as described in McGonigal's article "Museums as Happiness Pioneers," appear to be constant across different demographics and different countries, although each one may have a stronger or weaker emphasis for specific groups. The four principles are

- satisfying work
- experience at being good at something
- time spent with people we like
- the chance to be a part of something bigger

"If we have these four things, it really doesn't matter what is happening in our lives" (McGonigal 2009, 51). I agree.

Keeping this view in mind, it is evident that for older adults, using the four happiness principles as a basis for action can provide an alternative to and escape from the vicissitudes of the last third of life. These factors may include disappointment in relationships with family or friends or both; the loss of those relationships and people; ill health; changes in financial, work, and social status; and relocation.

APPLICATIONS

Librarians can be intentional in fostering feelings of hope and happiness. They are in the perfect position to initiate and support projects among older adults. They work in all communities with all social and cultural groups. They have neutral, trusted status (people reveal themselves to librarians in ways they do not to others). Thus, librarians are perfectly situated to make the successful connections between the individuals and groups needed to participate in collaborative projects. Integral to well-planned collaborative work are the four happiness principles: *satisfying work, being good at something, time spent with people we like,* and *the chance to be a part of something bigger than ourselves.* Librarians are perfectly positioned to implement these principles in libraries and in the multiplicity of settings where people live their lives. In fact some librarians use these principles unaware that they are doing so.

Because this discussion is meant to encourage librarians to create practical projects and activities, it may be useful to operationalize the concept with a story of one successful collaborative project for older adults. A new library building in a medium-sized older community was criticized for its modern architecture and cold feeling. A few library users complained about the lack of landscaping around the perimeter of the library. The librarian helped them form a group to research appropriate plants for the landscaping. The "gardeners" contacted the local state agricultural center as well as a nearby university botanical specialist to decide on plant selection. They worked out a landscape design using library resources. They involved others in the community in fund-raising and then organized an event—a planting day. At each juncture in the project, the librarian provided feedback. The library's board recognized the outstanding work of the group members by sponsoring a special event for them.

This successful collaborative project was initiated by a savvy librarian, attuned to the needs of the library users and their non-library-using friends. Although the project included adults of all ages, the older adults in the community took the lead and had the interest to ensure the success of the project. Clearly the project fulfilled their happiness needs. Anyone who writes long- or short-term plans—and librarians do this regularly—is familiar with the long lists of goals and objectives such plans generate. I am not sure that I have ever seen ensuring happiness as an overall goal. It should be!

I wonder to what extent I can expect this discussion of technology, brain research, and happiness to contribute to the future skills and knowledge of librarians in the year 2040. If we look to the past, we can find the answer in the originator of the Five Laws of Library Science, Ranganathan. If we look to the future, we can rely on the ideas and imagination of the participants in the 2006 Idaho Library Futures Conference.

REFERENCES

Cohen, G. 2006. *The mature mind.* New York: Perseus Books.

Goldberg, E., ed. 1990. *Contemporary neuropsychology and the legacy of Luria.* Hillsdale, NJ: Erlbaum. (This is a Festschrift to Luria.)

———. 2005. *The wisdom paradox: How your mind can grow stronger as your brain grows older.* New York: Gotham Books.

Idaho's Library Future 2006–2020. 2006. Vision 2020: Idaho Library Futures Conference— Challenges of the Future. http://libraries.idaho.gov/files/2020vision-document.pdf.

Kazdin, A., ed. 2000. *Encyclopedia of psychology.* New York: Oxford University Press.

McGonigal, J. 2009. Museums as happiness pioneers. *Museum,* March/April.

Pink, D. 2006. *A whole new mind: Why right-brainers will rule the future.* New York: Riverhead.

Ranganathan, S. R. 1931. *The Five Laws of Library Science.* Madras, India: Madras Library Association.

Sheehy, N. 2004. *Fifty key thinkers in psychology.* London: Routledge.

Contributors

Stephen Abram, MLS, was elected president of the Special Libraries Association (SLA) in 2008 and is vice president, strategic partnerships and markets, for Gale Cengage. He is a past president of the Canadian Library Association and an SLA fellow. He is also the past president of the Ontario Library Association and has served on the SLA board of directors as director and secretary. In June 2003 he was awarded SLA's John Cotton Dana Award and the University of Toronto's Jubilee Award. A leading international librarian and thinker in the North American library community, Abram has more than twenty-five years' experience in libraries and in the information industry. *Stephen's Lighthouse* is his blog on culture, history, technology, politics, economics, and more.

Stefan Agrigoroaei is a postdoctoral fellow in the Lifespan Developmental Psychology Lab at Brandeis University. He received his doctorate in 2007 from the University of Savoie, Chambéry, France. His general area of interest is the antecedents of memory beliefs and their influence on cognitive performance. Agrigoroaei's current work focuses on memory beliefs in a life-span perspective and, more precisely, on their experimental manipulations, and on the accuracy of memory self-assessments. He is also interested in other modifiable factors that can account for the interindividual and intraindividual variability in memory performance (e.g., cognitive, physical, and social activities).

Robert C. Atchley is Distinguished Professor of Gerontology (Emeritus) at Miami University in Oxford, Ohio, and a specialist on aging and spirituality. He is former chair of the Department of Gerontology at Naropa University, Boulder, Colorado, and has taught at George Washington University. Atchley has written over twenty-seven books, including *Social Forces in Aging,* the leading gerontology textbook, and *Spirituality and Aging: Expanding the View* (2008). He has contributed more than one hundred articles to professional journals under the name Bob Atchley. He helped launch the Scripps Gerontology Center and served as its director from 1974 to 1998. He is former president of the American Society on Aging and is a leading proponent of the "conscious aging" movement and related aspects of late-life activity.

Mary Catherine Bateson is a writer and cultural anthropologist who is currently a visiting scholar at Boston College's Center on Aging and Work. Her doctoral degree is from Harvard. She has been dean of the faculty at Amherst College, Clarence J. Robinson Professor in Anthropology and English at George Mason University, and visiting professor at the Harvard Graduate School of Education. She is currently exploring the ways in which lifelong learning modifies the rhythms of the life cycle and the interaction between generations. Bateson has written and coauthored numerous books and articles, including academic works on Arabic linguistics; *With a Daughter's Eye,* a memoir of her anthropologist parents, Margaret Mead and Gregory Bateson; *Composing a Life; Peripheral Visions: Learning Along the Way; Full Circles, Overlapping Lives: Culture and Generation in Transition;* and *Willing to Learn: Passages of Personal Discovery.* Her current project, *Composing a Further Life: The Age of Active Wisdom,* will appear in 2010.

Jessica Blum is a graduate student in Education Leadership Studies at Teachers College, Columbia University. She holds a BA and an MA in English Language and Literature from Emory University and Hofstra University, respectively, and returned to graduate study after nine years of rewarding experience as a teacher and leader in alternative education programs in New York and Ohio. Committed to studying and developing innovative leadership strategies, teaching tools, and growth-enhancing learning environments, Blum works in Teachers College's Library EdLab, a research, design, and development unit dedicated to the future of both libraries and the education sector. Blum will next pursue doctoral study in her area of professional interest.

Ellie Drago-Severson is an associate professor of Education Leadership at Teachers College, Columbia University. Her research interests include leadership development; supporting adults' professional and personal development in a variety of settings, including ABE/ESOL, libraries, K–12 schools, and university contexts; and qualitative research methods. Drago-Severson has written three books: *Becoming Adult Learners: Principles and Practices for Effective Development* (2004), *Helping Teachers Learn: Principal Leadership for Adult Growth and Development* (2004), and *Leading Adult Learning* (2009). *Helping Teachers Learn* recently won the National Staff Development Council's 2004 Book of the Year award. Drago-Severson's work focuses primarily on assisting teachers and leaders in a variety of contexts to support and nurture adult development.

Nan Kari is a cofounder of the Jane Addams School for Democracy, a civic engagement and democratic initiative for immigrant families and college students, located in the multicultural West Side of St. Paul, Minnesota. She coauthored *Building America: The Democratic Promise of Public Work* and, most recently, coedited *Voices of Hope: The Story of the Jane Addams School for Democracy.* She has many published articles and chapters on public engagement. Kari has led several initiatives in democratic renewal in a variety of settings. She is a senior associate at the Center for Democracy and Citizenship at the Humphrey Institute of Public Affairs at the University of Minnesota and a senior associate at the Touchstone Center for Collaborative Inquiry.

Miwako Kidahashi is a sociologist who has written on Japanese corporate culture. She has a doctoral degree from Columbia University. Her dissertation was *Dual Organization: A Study of a Japanese-Owned Firm in the United States.* She has been a visiting scholar at the Institute for Social and Economic Research and Policy at Columbia University.

Margie Lachman is professor and chair of the Department of Psychology, Brandeis University. Her research specialties are life-span development, midlife, sense of control, adult personality, memory, health-promoting behaviors, and intervention to improve cognitive and physical functioning. Her doctoral degree is from Pennsylvania State University. She received the Distinguished Research Achievement Award from the American Psychological Association, Division 20—Adult Development and Aging in 2003, and the Archstone Foundation Award for Excellence in Program Innovation in 1998. She is the author of numerous articles in professional journals, including "Daily Physical Activity: Relation to Everyday Memory in Adulthood" (*Journal of Applied Gerontology* 2008), "Perceptions of Aging in Two Cultures: Korean and American Views on Old Age" (*Journal of Cross-Cultural Gerontology* 2006), and "Aging Under Control?" (*Psychological Science Agenda* 2005).

R. David Lankes is director of the Information Institute of Syracuse and a professor in Syracuse University's School of Information Studies. He is the first fellow of ALA's Office for Information Technology Policy. He received his BFA (multimedia design), MS (Telecommunications), and PhD from Syracuse University. A winner of the 2009 Emerald Award, he has written, coauthored, and edited seven books and written over thirty book chapters as well as numerous articles. His books include *Virtual Reference Service: From Competencies to Assessment* (2009) and *Digital Reference in the New Millennium* (2000). He has been principal investigator for competitively awarded research totaling $13 million. Lankes is a sought-after keynote speaker around the globe. He writes the popular blog *Virtual Dave.*

Ronald J. Manheimer is executive director of the North Carolina Center for Creative Retirement (NCCCR), a lifelong learning, leadership, research, and community service program of the University of North Carolina, Asheville, where he also holds an appointment as research associate professor of philosophy. Manheimer was formerly director of older adult education for the National Council on Aging. He trained in philosophy, earning a PhD from the Board of Studies in History of Consciousness, University of California, Santa Cruz, and has taught at Wayne State University, the University of California, Santa Cruz, San Diego State University, The Evergreen State College, UNC-Asheville, and the Smithsonian. Manheimer has published numerous books and articles investigating philosophical issues of later life and human development, including *A Map to the End of Time: Wayfarings with Friends and Philosophers* (1999), *Older Americans Almanac: A Reference Work on Seniors in the United States* (1994), *The Second Middle Age: Looking Differently at Life Beyond 50* (1995), and *Older Adult Education: A Guide to Research, Policies and Programs* (1995).

Joanne Gard Marshall is an Alumni Distinguished Professor at the School of Information and Library Science at the University of North Carolina, Chapel Hill. She served as dean of the school from 1999 to 2004. Prior to 1999, Marshall was a faculty member at the University of Toronto. In addition to her PhD in public health, she holds a master of health science degree from McMaster University and a master of library science degree from McGill University. In 2005 she received an honorary doctorate of letters from McGill University. Before assuming her faculty appointment at the University of Toronto, Marshall worked for fifteen years as a librarian and has received a number of awards for her achievements in medical librarianship. She is currently conducting research on workforce issues in library and information science. Marshall also leads the North Carolina Collaboration on Lifelong Learning and Engagement project, which aims to support public libraries and other cultural institutions as they develop new initiatives to respond to changing demographic trends.

Victor Marshall is a professor of sociology at the University of North Carolina, Chapel Hill, and director of the university's Institute on Aging. He has also served as director of the Institute for Life Course and Aging at the University of Toronto. From 1990 to 1995 he was director of the Canadian Aging Research Network. Marshall is a fellow of the Gerontological Society of America and a founding member and former vice president of the Canadian Association on Gerontology. He currently serves on the editorial boards of *Ageing and Society, Journal of Aging and Health, Social Forces,* and the *Encyclopedia of Gerontology.* Marshall's published research has covered such diverse aspects of aging as the family, long-term care, migration, and death and dying. He is known for his work on the life course perspective, an approach that recognizes the complex mix of personal, social, historical, demographic, and other issues that affect the experience of aging. He led the United States WANE (Workforce Aging in the New Economy) research team and is currently coprincipal investigator for a study of the working life courses of library school graduates.

Stephen Ristau has more than thirty years' experience in the human services sector as an executive, senior manager, consultant and trainer, and clinician. He has served as president and CEO of four nonprofit human services organizations. His consulting firm, Ristau and Associates, provides public and nonprofit organizations with consultation and training services with an emphasis on organization and leadership development. His recent work has focused on expanding the connections between nonprofit organizations, purposeful work, and older Americans, especially the baby boom generation. Among other engagements, he is working with the California State Library on two statewide initiatives: Transforming Life after 50 and Get Involved: Powered By Your Library.

David Scheie, founder and president of the Touchstone Center for Collaborative Inquiry, is an evaluation consultant and learning facilitator. He works with nonprofit and community groups, foundations, and government agencies to clarify strategies, document results, and identify and use lessons for greater effectiveness. He specializes in collaborative, participatory approaches in which organizational leaders and other stakeholders are active in designing, implementing, and making meaning of evaluations. Scheie earned his PhD in organizational and community development from Union Institute and University. He is on the community faculty of Metropolitan State University in St. Paul, Minnesota, and a frequent presenter at evaluation conferences. His writing has appeared in *The Evaluation Exchange, Shelterforce, Challenge of Faith,* and *The Neighborhood Works.*

Selma Thomas is the founder and principal of Watertown Productions, Inc., a media design and production firm based in Washington, DC. A filmmaker with a background in history, Thomas produced several award-winning public television documentaries before beginning her work with museums and libraries. She has designed and produced electronic programs, both site- and web-based, for a variety of cultural institutions. Clients include the Smithsonian Institution, the National Museum of American History, the National Gallery of Art, the Children's Discovery Museum of San Jose (California), the Chicago History Museum, the Exploratorium, the Franklin Institute Science Museum, and the Library of Congress. A frequent author and speaker on the strategic and interpretive uses of media, Thomas is media editor of *Curator: The Museum Journal* and coeditor of and contributor to *The Virtual and the Real* (an exploration of the interpretive role of media in museums). She is the author of "Private Memory in Public Spaces: Oral History in the Museum" (*Oral History and Public Memories,* 2007).

Index